Malta & Gozo

DIRECTIONS

WRITTEN AND RESEARCHED BY

Victor Paul Borg

NEW YORK • LONDON • DELHI

www.roughguides.com

Contents

Introduction to Malta

With more historical monuments per square kilometre than anywhere else and a record number of World Heritage Sights for its size, Malta feels like a huge open-air museum. The impressive fortifications and buildings are a legacy of the chequered 7000-year-old history of Malta, Gozo and Comino – a history that has alternated between long spells of isolation and brief outbursts of momentousness, mostly during wars and periods of upheaval when Malta's strategic location at the centre of the Mediterranean gave the country a significance disproportionate to its diminutive size. These sights are complemented by a sunny climate, sparkling waters, some sandy beaches and top-notch modern Mediterranean food. The islands' quaintness and insularity are also part of the allure and – despite some lapses in services and infrastructure – Malta is a rewarding destination.

The majority of Malta's historical sights are concentrated in Valletta and the "Three Cities", laid out around the Grand Harbour and girdled by immense fortifications. Many of the impressive

◂ The Blue Grotto

▲ Għan Tuffieħa

churches and palaces within are characterized by exuberant Baroque architecture, which came courtesy of a grand makeover spearheaded by the Knights of Malta in the seventeenth and eighteenth centuries. There's also plenty of opportunity to get to grips with Malta's military past, with a host of impenetrable forts and several museums dedicated to the islands' crucial role during World War II. Though the extravagant designs of the Knights are ever-present, the Neolithic era made an equally significant mark on the islands. The magnificent temples scattered over Malta and Gozo – the

When to visit

Most people visit during the high season (May–Oct); in July and August, when the Maltese work less and go out more, things get pretty hectic. It's searingly hot, and the beaches are extremely crowded, but it's a lively time to visit, coinciding with the annual village *festas*. Rain is rare between May and September, and the countryside is parched and dry. Things get quieter in the low season (Oct–May): many hotels and guesthouses slash their prices and the tourist crowds disappear. The weather is mild (you'll usually be able to pick up a tan), rainfall occasional, and the countryside beautifully green, but the islands can feel somewhat melancholy, and the sea is far too cold for swimming. Outside of the high season, the best times to visit are the autumn or spring shoulder seasons. Sea swimming is pleasant up to December, while in the spring, the countryside is ablaze with wild flowers.

◀ Triq Ir-Repubblika, Valletta

oldest freestanding man-made structures in the world – are second to none, and there are more major complexes here than in the whole of the rest of Europe.

A short boat-ride from Malta, Gozo has a more rural character, going to sleep early and waking up with the roosters. And what it lacks in cultural sophistication and historical sights of the mainland, it makes up with tranquility, natural beauty and an amenable Mediterranean lifestyle. The hilly topography and ravishing coastal cliffs offer some marvellous walks, while the dive sites offshore are widely acknowledged as some of the best in the Mediterranean.

▶ The Citadel, Rabat, Gozo

Shifting prices

This guide was researched and written during Malta's changeover to the euro at the beginning of 2008 when all commercial enterprises and museums were required to show prices in both euros and Maltese lira. All businesses were prohibited from changing any prices during the switch, but the expectation is that prices will be rounded up eventually. Some restaurants were planning to change their menu, and to price the new items independently of the euro switchover, but most businesses will wait a few months until people get used to the euro before increasing their prices as part of a periodic price review. Therefore, many prices are likely to have shifted slightly – probably upwards – by the time you use this book.

Malta
AT A GLANCE

VALLETTA

The churches, convents, palaces and grand public buildings of Malta's capital, designated a World Heritage Site in its entirety, have remained largely unchanged since their construction more than 400 years ago. The addition of a clutch of national museums and art galleries, as well as Malta's best restaurants, make Valletta an eclectic place to explore.

▲ Valletta

MDINA

Mdina emerged as Malta's first urban settlement under Phoenician rule, but it was the Arabs who rebuilt the fortifications that you see today. The twisting alleys inside the citadel have kept vehicles and modernity at bay, and a ramble through this quiet area gives plenty of insight into the architectural whims of Malta's many rulers.

◄ Collachio, Vittoriosa

THREE CITIES

Characterized by a medieval urban fabric of close-knit Baroque architecture, the "Three Cities" of Vittoriosa, Senglea and Cospicua offer bags of atmosphere, and hold several absorbing sights, from imposing Knightly palaces and forts to museums dedicated to modern militaria.

◄ Mdina

◂ Mġar Harbour Gozo

WESTERN MALTA

With several sandy beaches and clear azure waters, many of them offering watersports facilities, western Malta is ideal for a day by the sea. Development has been relatively restrained here, and the landscape remains pleasantly natural. And if you're here in winter, the beaches beckon for bracing walks by the ocean.

▸ Mellieha Bay

◂ Capors in bloom, Comino

COMINO

The tiny islet of Comino boasts a couple of lovely places to swim, including the clear turquoise waters of the Blue Lagoon, as well as some scenic coastal walks. The best time to visit is in the spring, when the rocky garigue habitat comes spectacularly into bloom.

SOUTHEASTERN MALTA

The four Neolithic temples scattered around the southeast makes the area a must on any itinerary. All the temples are stylistically different, and most stunning is the Hypogeum, an underground shrine with a tangible air of mystery.

GOZO

With self-contained towns clustered around gigantic parish churches, and a population whose hospitality is legendary, Gozo offers a peaceful, pastoral alternative to Malta – and some stunning beaches and coastal landscapes, too.

◂ Haġar Qim Neolithic Temple

Ideas

The big six

Malta and Gozo's top sights are mostly the legacy of the islands' two "golden ages" – the Neolithic era, when the temple-building inhabitants were some of the most artistically advanced of their time, and the time of the Knights of Malta, who left an indelible mark with their immense fortifications and extravagant Baroque buildings.

▲ St John's Co-Cathedral

The former conventual church of the Knights of Malta is thick with their commemorative monuments.

P.53 ▸ VALLETTA AND FLORIANA

▲ Vittoriosa

The placid Dockyard Creek forms a perfect foreground for Vittoriosa's triumphalist Baroque architecture.

P.64 ▸ THE THREE CITIES

▶ St Paul's Cathedral

A grand architectural set-piece and the masterpiece of Malta's most famous architect, Lorenzo Gafa.

P.86 ▸ MDINA, RABAT AND THE SOUTH CENTRAL COAST

▼ The Citadel, Rabat

The fortified citadel that towers over Rabat retains a fantastic medieval fabric, and is home to Gozo's best museums.

P.136 ▸ GOZO

▲ Grand Master's Palace

Malta's seat of rule for more than 400 years, and a lasting testament to the wealthy Knights of Malta.

P.54 ▸ VALLETTA AND FLORIANA

▶ Hypogeum

With three underground levels bored into the rock by hand, the Hypogeum is one of the most fantastic monuments of the ancient world.

P.121 ▸ THE SOUTHEAST

Churches

With more than 350 churches – that's almost one church for every thousand inhabitants – Malta's distinction as the most devoutly Catholic country in the world is highly visible: each town is dominated by its grand Catholic church, many of which were built in the seventeenth century during a nationwide drive to create ornate Baroque edifices. Piercing the skyline island wide, the bell towers and domes of these churches serve as a characteristic part of any Maltese view.

▲ Gozo Cathedral

The highlight of the interior here is the trompe l'oeil ceiling painting.

P.136 ▸ GOZO

▲ St John the Baptist Church, Xewkija

One of Europe's largest churches, visible from most of Gozo and dwarfing the town of Xewkija.

P.138 ▸ GOZO

▲ Ta' Pinu Basilica

Set in open countryside, the Ta' Pinu is an arresting sight.

P.146 ▸ GOZO

▶ St Paul's Shipwreck Church

Dedicated to the saint who was shipwrecked in Malta, and with a couple of associated relics and outstanding works of art.

P.55 ▸ VALLETTA AND FLORIANA

▼ St John's Co-Cathedral

Italian artist Mattia Preti's intricate sculptures fill every crevice of the Co-Cathedral's interior.

P.53 ▸ VALLETTA AND FLORIANA

Fortress Malta

Malta's strategic position in the centre of the Mediterranean made it a valuable stepping stone, and the various regional powers that have occupied the island over the last 2000 years have turned it into a veritable citadel state. The most impressive defences are the great fortifications erected by the Knights.

▲ Valletta's fortifications

Studded with sentry posts, the fortifications that girdle Valletta are undeniably impressive.

P.47 ▸ VALLETTA AND FLORIANA

▲ St Mary's Tower

Malta's largest coastal tower, built here to protect vessels crossing between Malta and Gozo against pirate attacks.

P.156 ▸ COMINO

▲ Fort St Angelo

Malta's most famous fort has faithfully guarded the Grand Harbour since 1200 AD.

P.68 ▸ THE THREE CITIES

◀ Cottonera Lines

Pierced by the ornate Notre Dame Gate, Malta's largest defensive wall took fifty years to build.

P.69 ▸ THE THREE CITIES

▼ 100-ton gun, Fort Rinella

Installed to defend the sea routes into the Grand Harbour, this is the largest cannon ever made.

P.70 ▸ THE THREE CITIES

Festivals

Most Maltese festivals arise from the country's intense Catholicism. The majority of them are held in the summer when the Maltese work less and go out more, and they culminate in the grand town feasts, which are colourful and passionate events. The off-season is quieter, but not without its highlights: Christmas, Carnival in February, and the Good Friday re-enactments in April break up the monotony of winter.

▲ Carnival

Traditional bands in bars and hilarious street performances work up a storm of revelry in Nadur.

P.167 ▸ ESSENTIALS

▼ Feast fireworks

The displays staged during the town feasts, in honour of their parish saint, feature some of the best and most original pyrotechnic set pieces in the world.

P.165 ▸ ESSENTIALS

Notte Bianca – Lejl Imdawwal

Concerts are just some of the various events that attract thousands to Valletta for the night-long cultural activities.

P.167 ▸ ESSENTIALS

Christmas

Sumptuous decor and creative cribs, especially in Gozo, add a colourful and religious aspect to Christmas celebrations.

P.168 ▸ ESSENTIALS

Good Friday procession

Good Friday sees hooded penitents parade through the streets.

P.167 ▸ ESSENTIALS

Beaches

Although the islands have relatively few sandy beaches, which means that they can get very crowded in summer, quality makes up for quantity, with gorgeous swathes of sand set in gloriously natural landscapes – and you can beat the crowds by swimming in the mornings. If you're happy to forego sand, you'll find many scenic bays and gorges cut into the rocky coastline which offer clear, inviting waters.

▲ Għajn Tuffieħa

Fantastic cliffs, amber sands and clear water make this one of Malta's most attractive beaches.

P.96 › MDINA, RABAT AND THE SOUTH CENTRAL COAST

◀ **Ramla Bay**

One of the Mediterranean's most scenic beaches, great for a winter stroll or a summer swim.

P.145 ▸ GOZO

▶ **Blue Lagoon**

This sweep of clear azure water is best enjoyed in the mornings, before the invasion of touring boats.

P.153 ▸ COMINO

▼ **San Blas Bay**

This small sandy beach remains gloriously untouched, fringed by bamboo and tamarisk trees and backed by citrus groves.

P.145 ▸ GOZO

◀ **Peter's Pool**

A dramatically eroded rocky shoreline and clear greenish waters make this spot a popular draw.

P.130 ▸ THE SOUTHEAST

Knights' Malta

The Knights that ruled Malta for over 350 years were volunteer Christian crusaders who hailed from the cream of Europe's aristocracy. Each knight's family had to bequeath two-thirds of their annual income to the organization, while the assets of individual knights were inherited by the brotherhood upon their death – which made Malta's Knights fabulously wealthy. Their lifestyles were hugely extravagant, and their military might legendary.

▲ National Museum of Fine Arts

Antoine de Favray's portraits of knights illustrate their penchant for pomp and vanity.

P.51 ▸ VALLETTA AND FLORIANA

▲ Grand Master's Palace

The Knights' grand military victory is retold via outstanding frescoes depicting episodes of the Great Siege of 1565.

P.54 ▸ VALLETTA AND FLORIANA

▲ Maritime Museum

The Knights' military might is explained in numerous exhibits here.

P.68 ▸ THE THREE CITIES

▼ Auberge de Castille

The Knights' largest inn of residence, and Malta's grandest secular Baroque building.

P.47 ▸ VALLETTA AND FLORIANA

▲ The Armoury

The impressive range of military hardware amassed by the Knights is displayed at the Armoury.

P.54 ▸ VALLETTA AND FLORIANA

Restaurants

With French and Italian culinary influences, and more recently inspired by East–West fusion cooking as well, Malta's restaurant scene is eclectic. Increasingly, the best restaurants offer inventive, constantly evolving Mediterranean food, using classic Maltese ingredients such as rabbit or octopus to produce some original and appealing menus.

▼ Ta Frenċ

A rustic setting, an impressive wine cellar, and creative French cuisine make this Gozo's best restaurant.

P.155 ▸ GOZO

▼ Rubino

Rubino's ever-changing menu of seasonal dishes continues to set the standard for modern Maltese cuisine.

P.62 ▸ VALLETTA AND FLORIANA

▲ **Malata**

Memorable French cuisine in an enviable location in front of the Grand Master's Palace.

P.62 ▸ VALLETTA AND FLORIANA

▼ **It-Tmun**

Gozo's long-established option for fusion food remains an old favourite.

P.154 ▸ GOZO

◀ **Terrazza**

Great Mediterranean food served on a terrace with lovely views of romantic Spinola Bay.

P.80 ▸ SLIEMA AND ST JULIAN'S

Neolithic Malta

With the most extensive concentration of Neolithic temples in the world, five of which are designated World Heritage Sites, Malta and Gozo's Neolithic remains are unparalleled, and constitute the oldest free-standing man-made structures anywhere on the globe. The islands are also the source of the world's largest and most artistically accomplished cache of Neolithic sculptures known as "fat ladies".

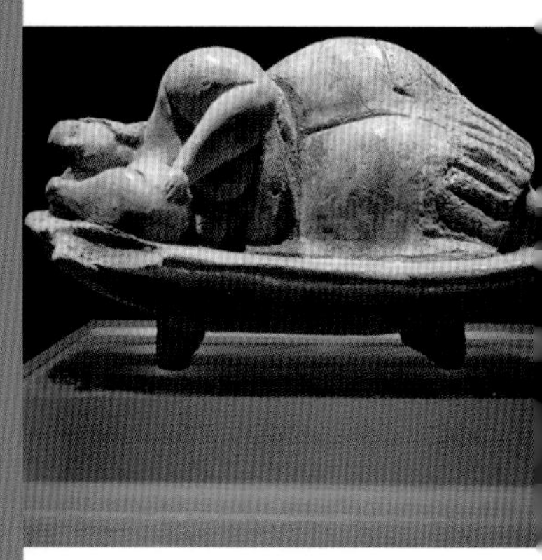

▲ "Fat lady" statues

These beautiful figures serve as an eloquent reminder of the artistic achievements of Malta's Neolithic peoples.

P.52 ▸ VALLETTA AND FLORIANA

▲ Clapham Junction cart ruts

These deep channels are one of Malta's most intractable archeological mysteries.

P.94 ▸ MDINA, RABAT AND THE SOUTH CENTRAL COAST

▲ **Ġgantija temple**

Despite being built some 5600 years ago, the temple complex here remains surprisingly intact.

P.143 ▸ GOZO

▶ **Mnajdra temple**

Set on round stones, the many altars at Mnajdra are unique to this temple.

P.127 ▸ THE SOUTHEAST

▼ **Ħaġar Qim**

The heavy trilithon entrance here is one of the temple's most elegant features.

P.127 ▸ THE SOUTHEAST

Architecture

Although Malta's various foreign rulers have left some glorious edifices, the islands' location has been the chief influence on their architecture. Ornate, Italian-style Baroque dominates, and is nicely expressed in many beautiful stone balconies. Styles intermingle in other cases, especially in the Siculo-Norman architecture, equally influenced by Sicilian peasant houses and Norman touches.

▲ Rabat old town

The anonymous and meandering alleyways are littered with delightful Baroque features and niches of saints.

P.134 ▸ GOZO

▲ Manoel Theatre

Malta's national theatre is notable for its intricate Baroque interior.

P.57 ▸ VALLETTA AND FLORIANA

▲ Għarb balconies

The fantastic stone balconies here, many of which incorporate Catholic motifs, provide a quaint taste of rural Baroque.

P.148 ▸ GOZO

▼ Valletta balconies

Enclosed timber balconies grace many old houses in Malta, but are ubiquitous in Valletta.

P.47 ▸ VALLETTA AND FLORIANA

▲ Inquisitors' Palace

The courtyard here boasts a rare example of a Rhodesian Gothic cross-ribbed ceiling.

P.65 ▸ THE THREE CITIES

World War II Malta

Despite being the most heavily bombed country during World War II, Malta's civilian casualties were kept relatively low due to an extensive system of underground bunkers that housed the entire population. Nonetheless, food shortages brought the islands to the brink of surrender, but the nation's perseverance was eventually rewarded when Malta was decorated with the George Cross, Britain's highest award for acts of gallantry – the only time it has been awarded to a whole nation.

▲ Unexploded bomb, Mosta Dome

This lucky escape serves as a reminder of the war and has entered local Catholic mythology.

P.101 › CENTRAL MALTA

▼ Lascaris War Rooms

This absorbing museum includes an exhibition of the invasion of Sicily that was engineered and launched from Malta.

P.50 › VALLETTA AND FLORIANA

▲ Siege Bell Monument

The tolling of this huge bell commemorates the 7000 people who died in Malta during the war.

P.55 ▸ VALLETTA AND FLORIANA

▼ War Museum

The exhibits here provide a detailed background on Malta during the war.

P.56 ▸ VALLETTA AND FLORIANA

▼ Floriana War Memorial

This striking and unusual statue commemorates Britain's Royal Air Force war casualties.

P.59 ▸ VALLETTA AND FLORIANA

Dead Malta

For Malta's devoutly religious population, from early Christians to contemporary Catholics, death is regarded as the harbinger of eternal glory following a life of sacrifice. Passing on is a celebratory occasion here, as is apparent with the lavishly opulent tombs of the islands' cemeteries – the wealthy are often buried in mini-mausoleums.

▼ Archeology Museum

The exhibits here give an interesting insight into burial traditions over the centuries.

P.137 › GOZO

▼ Addolorata Cemetery

Malta's largest cemetery offers a fascinating look into local attitudes to death.

P.122 › THE SOUTHEAST

▲ Caravaggio's Beheading of St John the Baptist

Considered one of the premier canvases of the seventeenth century, Caravaggio's masterpiece is breathtaking.

P.54 ▸ VALLETTA AND FLORIANA

► Tombstones, St John's Co-Cathedral

Death, triumph and glory set in inlaid marble.

P.53 ▸ VALLETTA AND FLORIANA

▼ St Paul's Catacombs

Over a thousand sarcophagi hollowed underground provide a spooky insight of the burial practices of early Christians.

P.92 ▸ MDINA, RABAT, AND THE SOUTH CENTRAL COAST

Walks

If you stray from the nearest car park or settlement for a short stroll, you'll find that the Maltese islands offer some truly spectacular vistas, whether over the rugged undeveloped interior or the scenic coastline. The serrated clay slopes and cliffs of the southern coasts offer the most dramatic walking territory in Malta, whilst Gozo boasts a gorgeous landscape of table-top hills, as well as the unusual backdrop of its saltpans.

▲ **Ras Il-Qammiegħ**

The rugged garigue landscape, and views of serrated coastal cliffs, is best appreciated on foot.

P.114 › THE NORTHWEST

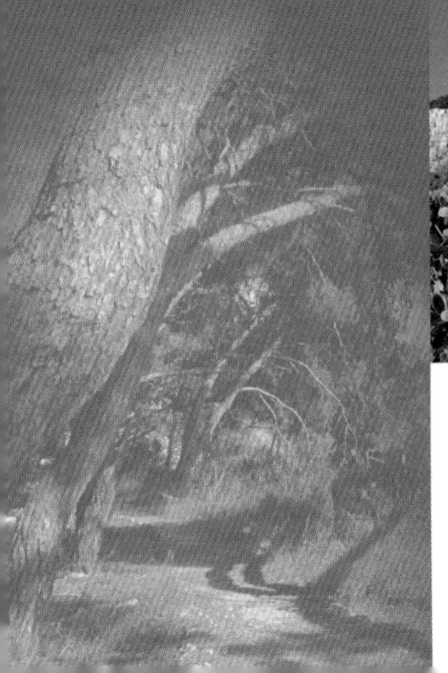

▲ **Ġordan Hill**

A country ramble in Gozo's western hills reveals the diversity of rural wildlife, especially in winter when the landscape is green.

P.147 › GOZO

▼ Il-Kunċizzjoni

One of Malta's highest and least inhabited regions, offering fine views over western Malta and some rewarding strolls.

P.95 ▸ MDINA, RABAT AND THE SOUTH CENTRAL COAST

▲ Il-Buskett

With its gnarled pines and towering oaks, Malta's only mature woodland makes for a nice stroll.

P.94 ▸ MDINA, RABAT AND THE SOUTH CENTRAL COAST

◀ Xwejni saltpans

Take a walk among the wonderfully abstract patterns of Gozo's saltpans.

P.141 ▸ GOZO

Maltese food

There are few true Maltese dishes, as many of the classic offerings are actually variations of recipes that originated elsewhere – the traditional preparations of rabbit have French influences, while *pastizzi* hail from the Middle East. However, the Maltese incarnation of Mediterranean dishes has produced some unique concoctions.

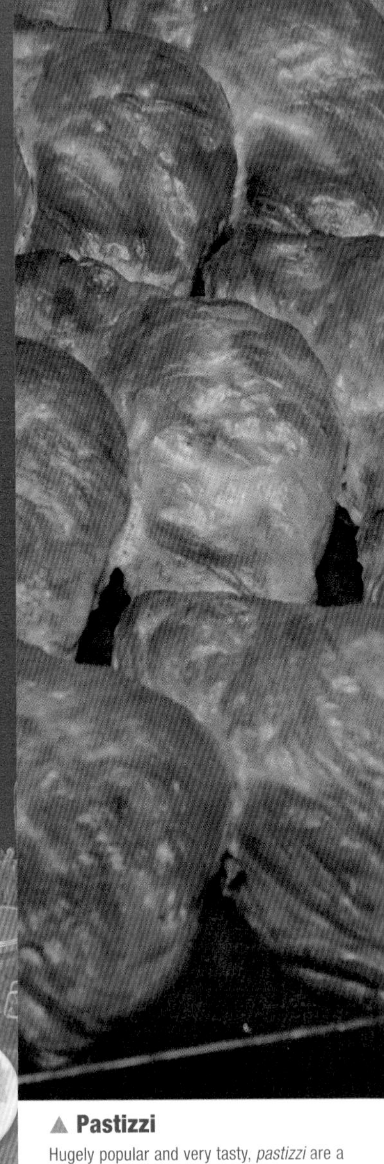

▲ **Pastizzi**

Hugely popular and very tasty, *pastizzi* are a great tea-time snack.

P.97 ▸ MDINA, RABAT AND THE SOUTH CENTRAL COAST

▲ **Gozitan antipasti**

Featuring locally made sausages and cheeses, Gozitan antipasti are pungent and hearty.

P.155 ▸ GOZO

▼ **Fresh bread**

Dense and crunchy, Malta's bread is excellent and addictive.

P.78 ▸ SLIEMA AND ST JULIAN'S

◀ **Rabbit**

Often invoked as Malta's national dish, rabbit cooked in the traditional Maltese style makes a wholesome meal.

P.116 ▸ THE NORTHWEST

▼ **Ftira**

Cooked in a wood-fired oven, these traditional Gozitan pizzas are a real treat.

P.155 ▸ GOZO

Views

From some of the islands' highest points you can appreciate both the architectural patterns of the towns, which expand in concentric circles from central squares with their Catholic churches, and countryside views of fields interspersed with natural habitats formed over millennia of human use, as well as more wild and rugged rocky plateaux and cliffs.

▲ Grand Harbour

The medieval cityscape that surrounds the harbour is best appreciated from Valletta's fortifications.

P.49 ▸ VALLETTA AND FLORIANA

▲ Sliema

Tumbling down the hillside and lapped by yacht-filled waters, Sliema asserts the picturesque side of Malta's modern development.

P.72 ▸ SLIEMA AND ST JULIAN'S

◀ Calypso's Cave

Ramla Valley, which cuts deep across high plateaux, is the most scenic of the island's valleys.

P.144 ▸ GOZO

▲ Citadel, Rabat

The view from Gozo's second-highest point reveals the hilly landscape and self-contained towns of Gozo's western region.

P.136 ▸ GOZO

▼ Mdina's ramparts

The ramparts here offer an eye-stretching view that takes in inland Malta and the Mosta Dome.

P.84 ▸ MDINA, RABAT AND THE SOUTH CENTRAL COAST

Bars and cafés

The clement Maltese climate ensures that outdoor cafés flourish throughout the islands, many of them atmospherically situated within historic towns. There's plenty of variety, too, with sophisticated wine bars or modern drinking holes offering music and entertainment, as well as colonial-era corner cafés and traditional town-square places that are often attached to local community groups such as bands and clubs.

▲ Il Gattopardo

Spread over several rooms and courtyards of an atmospheric Mdina house, this is a soothing and artsy spot for a drink.

P.97 ▸ MDINA, RABAT AND THE SOUTH CENTRAL COAST

▲ Juuls

Sophisticated by Paċeville standards, and playing an excellent mix of music.

P.82 ▸ SLIEMA AND ST JULIAN'S

▲ Café Jubilee

Warm ambience, tasteful music and good snacks make this a Valletta favourite.

P.61 ▸ VALLETTA AND FLORIANA

▶ The Fortress

Set in an old fortress, this bar serves tasty platters for sharing, and a good selection of wines.

P.117 ▸ THE NORTHWEST

▼ Simon's Pub

The combination of delicious, inexpensive drinks and friendly staff is a real winner.

P.83 ▸ SLIEMA AND ST JULIAN'S

Seaside Malta

You're never far from the sea in Malta, and the coast is where most people play and relax. The many bars and restaurants built close to the sea provide a lovely setting for a meal or a drink, while the numerous promenades that are the focus of coastal towns offer a great vantage point to watch the comings and goings of the colourful local fishing boats, or join the locals for an evening stroll by the sea.

▲ **Passiġġata**

Join the locals in a slow evening stroll by the sea.

P.72 ▸ SLIEMA AND ST JULIAN'S

▲ **Marsaxlokk**

Filled with colourful Baroque boats, the harbour here is a beautiful sight.

P.129 ▸ THE SOUTHEAST

◀ Ras Il-Bajda, Xlendi

The sheer cliffs that girdle the great gulf at the mouth of Xlendi Bay are a dramatic sight.

P.140 ▸ GOZO

▲ Spinola Bay

With a host of restaurants fringing the bay, this is a great spot for a romantic waterside dinner.

P.73 ▸ SLIEMA AND ST JULIAN'S

▶ Grand Harbour boat trip

A trip aboard one of Malta's vernacular boats offers a lovely perspective of the fortified medieval towns that ring the Grand Harbour.

P.49 ▸ THE THREE CITIES

Malta outdoors

There are many opportunities to enjoy Malta's rugged, cliff-dominated coastline, whether sitting in a canoe or climbing the cliffs themselves, and the underwater topography around the islands makes it one of the best scuba diving destinations in the Mediterranean. Malta's location in the centre of the Mediterranean also means that it's a staging post for migratory birds, and Gozo's rural traditions can be enjoyed by spending a day getting your hands dirty at a farm.

▼ Hands-on farming

Get to grips with Gozo's rural character by spending a day working on a farm.

P.170 ▸ ESSENTIALS

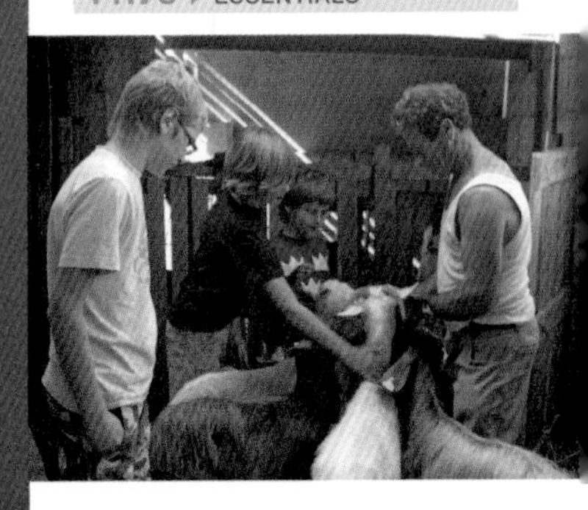

▼ Rock climbing

Innumerable cliffs offer all grades and types of rock climbing, from sports climbing to deep-water soloing.

P.170 ▸ ESSENTIALS

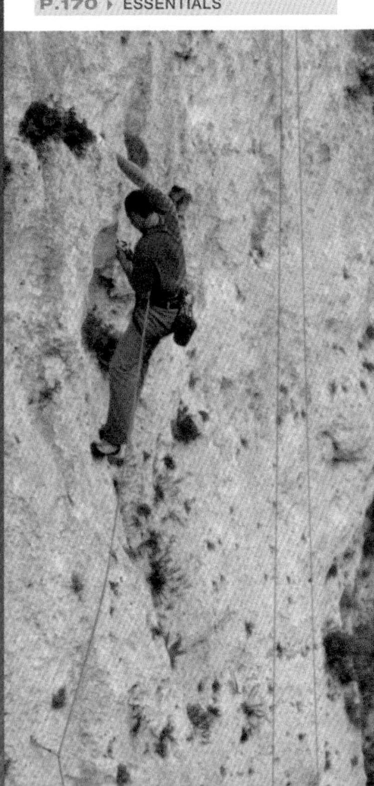

▲ Canoeing

The scenic north coast of Gozo, characterized by rocky bluffs towering over large bays, is best appreciated from a canoe.

P.149 ▸ GOZO

◀ Marine life

Colourful soft coral, clear water and fantastic underwater formations make Malta one of the top scuba-diving spots in the Mediterranean.

P.168 ▸ ESSENTIALS

▼ Birdwatching

Blue rock thrushes, Malta's national bird, is the most impressive of Malta's resident birds, but during spring and autumn migrations you can also see more exotic species.

P.170 ▸ ESSENTIALS

Places

Valletta and Floriana

Standing on the peninsula that divides Malta's largest two harbours, Valletta, Malta's impenetrable Baroque capital, was built by the Knights of Malta after they vanquished the Ottoman invasion in the Great Siege of 1565. A ring of grand fortifications enclose the tight grid of narrow streets full of churches, palaces and old buildings that have earned the town a well-deserved place on UNESCO's World Heritage list. The outstanding cathedral and Knights' former palace head a list of eclectic sights that include Malta's best museums and art galleries, and some of its finest restaurants. The town is also the island's commercial hub, and holds the largest concentration of shops. Floriana, overwhelmed by its illustrious neighbour, holds little of interest other than its impressive tiered fortifications and the grand setting of its town square.

Auberge de Castille

Pjazza Kastilja, Valletta. Dominating the lofty, traffic-swamped square that marks Valletta's highest point, the Auberge de Castille is the largest and most impressive of Valletta's four surviving *auberges* (inns for regional groups of Knights), a monumental Baroque building that stands as a reminder of the superiority of the Knights of Castille, one of the brotherhood's largest chapters. Though designed in the 1570s by Ġirolmu Cassar in the austere style the Knights then preferred, it was rebuilt in grand Baroque during the eighteenth century. It now occupies a whole block, with elaborate shell ornamentation framing

Visiting Valletta and Floriana

All buses to and from Valletta terminate at the bus station outside the city walls. There are no bus services inside the walls, but the town is small enough to see on foot. There are, however, small mini-cabs akin to golf karts, which operate from 8am to 8pm; if you can't see one to flag down, you can call ☎21/333321 or ☎79333321 (prices start from €1.05 for a single passenger). If you're driving you can park in the multi-storey car park near the bus station for a fee (prices vary depending on time, averaging €2 per hour), or use the free park-and-ride service – the car park, signposted in major approaches to Valletta, is just outside Floriana, and mini-buses shuttle commuters between here and Valletta's Freedom Square every few minutes from 6am to 1am. From Sliema, commuter boats make the 5-minute journey to Il-Mandraġġ on the western flank of Valletta (daily: May–Sept 7.45am–6.15pm; Oct–April 8.15am–5.45pm; every 30min or hour, depending on the time of day), and from Vittoriosa there are water taxis from in front of St Lawrence Church to Customs House on Valletta's eastern shore (9am–8pm; €5 for a single traveller, or €2.50 per person for two or more sharing).

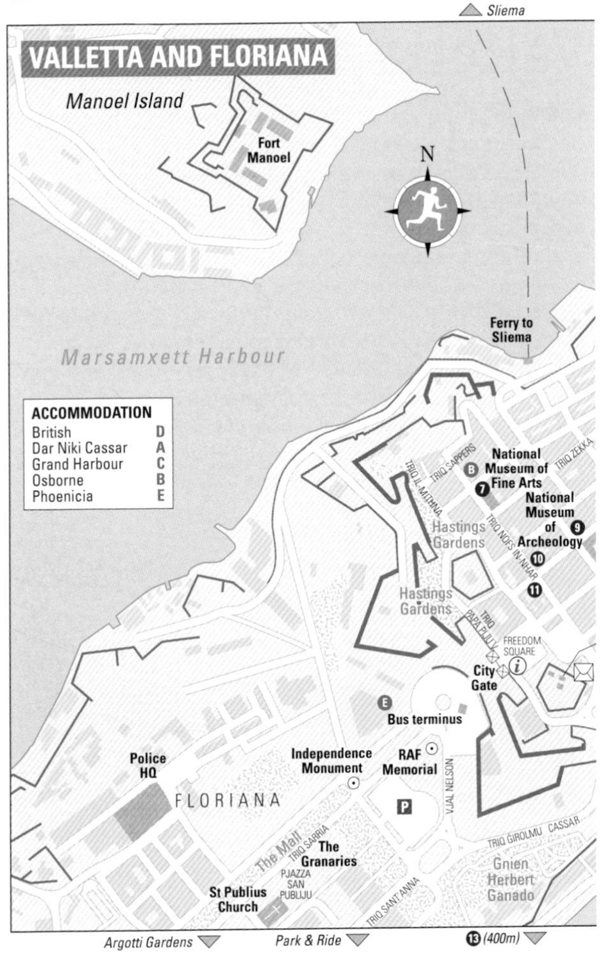

its continuous series of louvred windows; the large column-framed doorway is topped with a bust of Grand Master de Fonseca, who initiated the rebuilding. Fonseca's coat of arms is alongside that of the *Langue*, and is surrounded by a triumphant assembly of flags, swords, drums and shells. The *auberge* now houses the prime minister's office, and isn't open to the public.

Upper Barakka Gardens and the Saluting Battery

Pjazza Kastilja, Valletta. Daily 7.30am–dusk. Free. Set high behind the ramparts of Valletta's fortifications, this small garden – sprinkled with flower-beds, trees, pines and memorials – was created in 1661 by the Italian knight Flaminio Balbiani as a retreat for the Knights. Much of it, including its arcaded section, is the original design (the

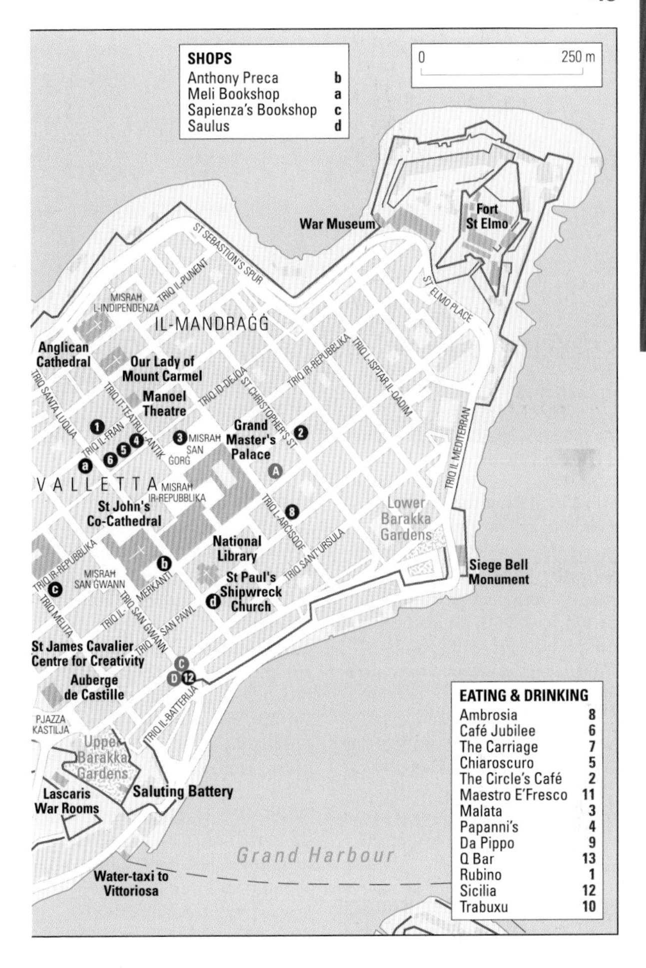

arcaded section was originally roofed, but when dissident Knights were meeting here in 1775 to plot against Grand Master Ximenes de Texada, he ordered the roof stripped off as a symbolic warning). The garden still provides a refuge from the street bustle, but the main reason to visit is for the **panoramic view** from Valletta's highest point: a vista taking in the breadth of the Grand Harbour, including the fantastic medieval townscape and the fortifications of the Three Cities (see p.64).

The **Saluting Battery** spreads over a series of chambers that once served as ammunition stores and a large terrace below the garden (accessed from within the garden or from Triq Il-Batterija; daily 9am–5pm; ☎21/225277; €4.70). Today it holds a display of virtually all kinds of

▲ UPPER BARAKKA GARDENS

weaponry from the 300 years it was an artillery battery for protecting the Grand Harbour, including an anti-aircraft gun that was installed on the terrace in World War II. Guided tours, on the hour, provide plenty of intriguing details, and two films are shown in rotation: one on the history of time, and another about the history of the Saluting Battery. At noon and sunset every day a cannon is fired as a salute – resurrecting a practice dating from the British period.

▼ BAROQUE FACADE, VALLETTA

Lascaris War Rooms

Lascaris Bastion, Valletta ⓣ21/234936. Mon–Fri 9.30am–4pm, Sat & Sun 9.30am–12.30pm. €4. Originally used by the Knights as living quarters for their slaves, this dank and mouldy underground complex gouged deep into the bedrock was converted into the British forces' Maltese centre of operations and the headquarters of the Royal Navy's Mediterranean Fleet during World War II. Conditions were claustrophobic – a thousand people worked here, 240 at a time in six-hour shifts – but it was from Lascaris that the Allies changed the course of the war in the Mediterranean by severely disrupting the Axis supplies to North Africa, launching the invasion of Sicily, and eventually engineering Italy's surrender. An interesting museum now re-creates the wartime atmosphere with wax dummies, maps, props and examples of weaponry such as the J-type Contact Mines that the Italians planted around Malta's seas. Each room is dedicated to an area of operation; the largest concentrates on Operation Husky, the 1943 Allied invasion of Sicily directed by General Dwight Eisenhower, where a large map of Sicily details the multi-pronged attack by air and sea. Entry to Lascaris War Rooms is either from Triq Ġirolmu Cassar or Triq San Anton (from the latter, follow the signs from outside Upper Barakka Gardens).

St James Cavalier Centre for Creativity

Triq Papa Piju V, Valletta ⓣ21/223200, ⓦwww.sjcav.org. Daily 10am–9pm. Free. Malta's national centre for modern arts occupies the historic site of St James Cavalier, an imposing pentagonal tower built in the 1570s to serve as a rearguard defence position, towering over the landward fortifications. Within its thick walls are a series of half-barrel ammunition chambers connected to a ramp that leads to the roof (where heavy guns used to be installed). The complex was converted into an arts centre in 1995 by Richard England, Malta's most famous contemporary architect, and the eleven former ammunition chambers now stage temporary art exhibitions in all media by Maltese and international artists. Although the shows are consistently good, there is often a hiatus between exhibitions – but the building is worth a visit in its own right. Moreover, on weekends between October and May English-language plays and occasional musicals and dance events are staged in the theatre-in-the-round, while the small cinema shows two art-house films each evening all year round; check the website for upcoming events and films.

Hastings Gardens

Triq Papa Piju V, Valletta. Daily 7.30am–dusk. Free. This diminutive garden set behind Valletta's fortifications is dedicated to Lord Hastings, a former British governor (1824–26) who died at sea in 1827 and is buried in the Neoclassical shrine at the centre of the garden. Small oaks, pines and sparse flowerbeds leave Hastings quite exposed, but its lofty viewpoints are reason enough to visit. You can see how the fortifications crease over each other to give a 180-degree fire-range; beyond there's Marsamxett Harbour with its yacht marinas, then Manoel Island and the conurbation of Sliema and St Julian's.

National Museum of Fine Arts

Triq Nofs In-Nhar, Valletta ⓣ21/225769, ⓦwww.heritagemalta.org. Daily 9am–5pm. €2.33. Originally the home of a French knight, and later the residence of the naval chief commander under the British, this Baroque and Rococo palace now houses a fine collection of paintings, mostly by Malta-associated artists. The building's large rooms have been pared down over the centuries, and little remains of the original splendour suggested by the grand staircase and fanciful Rococo ceiling-friezes. The exhibits date from the fourteenth to the twentieth centuries, and most deal with religious subjects. There are dozens of absorbing paintings – look out, particularly, for the various paintings by Mattia Preti, the Italian artist courted by the Knights whose work features in many Maltese churches; the solemn portraits of knights and other luminaries by the French artist Antoine de Favray; the dramatic depictions of monumental historical and religious events by Maltese artist Ġiuseppi Cali, and, on a different note, Edward Lear's charming pastel renditions of Maltese landscapes and townscapes painted during his visit in 1866.

National Museum of Archeology

Triq Ir-Repubblika, Valletta ⓣ21/221623, ⓦwww.heritagemalta.org. Daily 9am–7pm. €2.33. Built in 1575 to a design by Girolmu Cassar, the former Auberge de Provence now houses the National Museum of Archeology whose rich array of exhibits, dating from 5000 to 2500 BC, represent the legacy of the Neolithic era's most advanced nation. The collection is exhibited chronologically, starting from a model of a rock-cut tomb of the Żebbuġ Phase and incised pottery and pendants of rodents' teeth from the Għar Dalam and Skorba Phases, displayed in the first room. Things get more dramatic in the neighbouring Tarxien Hall, full of spiral motifs carved on stones (thought to symbolize a worldview of cyclical continuity) that were removed from the Tarxien temple and, more importantly, a hollowed altar in which animal bones and flint knives were found – the strongest evidence of animal sacrifices in Malta's temples. Next, the Prehistoric Architecture room looks at the bigger picture, detailing how the temples were built – there's even a stone model dating from the temple-building period. Considered to be the first ever architectural design, it displays some of the features that make Maltese temples such robust structures: the large corner megaliths that provided support and the corbelling leading up to the primitive domed roofs. But the most stirring displays are in the Human Figure room, including stone phallic symbols and various human sculptures, thought to have been made for ceremonial use, consisting of a cluster of well-endowed female nudes and sexless figures with pleated skirts and headdresses. Some are headless, suggesting that different heads were affixed to the loop at the neck for different ceremonies. The museum's star exhibit, the "sleeping lady", is a hand-sized figurine unearthed from the

▼ NATIONAL MUSEUM OF FINE ARTS

▲ NEOLITHIC CARVED SPIRALS, NATIONAL MUSEUM OF ARCHEOLOGY

Hypogeum and depicting a large woman reclining on a couch; delicately carved in minute detail, her body's tranquil pose could be at temporary or eternal rest.

St John's Co-Cathedral and Museum

Triq Ir-Repubblika, Valletta ☎21/220536. Mon–Fri 9.30am–4.30pm, Sat 9.30am–1pm. €5.80. One of the world's most opulent churches, the Co-Cathedral is a legacy of the Knights' wealth, vanity and self-aggrandizement. It was designed by the prolific Ġirolmu Cassar in the 1570s to serve as their conventual church, and the austere facade, with its turret-like bell towers, reflects their early battle sensibilities. In the latter half of the seventeenth century, however, the Knights set about transforming the plain interior into a blaze of Baroque art. The Italian artist Mattia Preti (1613–99) supervised the twenty-year project, which in some years cost more than Malta's entire military budget.

The makeover scheme was conceived and carried out during the tenure of the Cotoner brothers – who ruled as Grand Masters from 1660 and 1680 – and whose coat of arms is mounted high on the pillars (the cotton tree it features represents the cotton-growing estate they hailed from). Most of the other artworks in the cavernous nave are the work of Preti, who was also responsible for several of the altar paintings. The **nave** is overwhelming – the pillars are ablaze with frothy leaf carvings and representations of the Maltese Cross, while the eighteen lurid vignettes on the vault, depicting episodes from St John's life, took Preti five years to complete (painting directly on the concave ceiling, he had to tinker carefully with the perspective so that the view from the ground wouldn't be distorted). The floor of the nave, meanwhile, has 364 inlaid marble tombs of influential knights: each features a Latin eulogy and epitaph framed by symbols of prestige and glory.

The artistic diversity of the Co-Cathedral was further enhanced when **eight side-chapels** were individually assigned to each *Langue*, or

Knightly regional grouping – each installed monuments to its regional Grand Masters and competed to create the most flamboyant decoration. There's further rich ornamentation to the right of the chancel in the chapel dedicated to Our Lady of Carafa, which is enclosed by silver balustrades and holds an elegant gilded icon of the Madonna. The crypt – where Grand Master La Vallette is interred in a stone sarcophagus – is the only part of the church that retains the original monastic simplicity.

Yet it's Oratory of St John that holds the most valuable relic: the **Beheading of St John the Baptist**, Caravaggio's magnificent masterpiece painted in 1608. A stunning achievement for its time, many art historians consider it the best painting of the seventeenth century given its grim realism, excellent composition and virtuoso use of light and shade.

▼ TRIQ SAN PAWL

The oratory itself – also full of dense carvings and motifs – is the work of Preti.

Beyond the oratory, a wing of the complex is now a **museum** that showcases the church's moveable art: heaps of silverware and vestments, various portraits of Knights and three huge and majestic Flemish tapestries, dating from 1702 and costing almost as much as an annual military budget, that were formerly hung in the Co-Cathedral's nave.

Grand Master's Palace and the Armoury

Misraħ San Ġorġ, Valletta ⓣ21/249349, ⓦwww.heritagemalta.org. An imposing two-storey building occupying an entire block, the Grand Master's Palace (Mon–Wed & Fri 10am–4pm, Sat & Sun 9am–5pm; closed occasionally during official state visits and other special events; €4.66) has served as Malta's seat of government since it was built to a design by Ġirolmu Cassar in 1571. Originally the residence of the Grand Master, then of British governors, it now houses the president's office and Maltese parliament. Its high bare exterior walls indicate the siege mentality prevalent in Cassar's time, but the interior is awash with artistic treasures accumulated over the centuries.

The **five state rooms** open to visitors are arranged around a U-shaped corridor that's decorated with geometric ceiling friezes, the Grand Master's marble coats of arms inlaid into the floors and a series of lunettes depicting knightly naval battles and idealized Maltese scenes. The State Rooms are richer: all feature dramatic thick-coffered and panelled timber ceilings with gilded pendants, massive crystal chandeliers, bold-coloured brocade fabrics, portraits of various Grand Masters and impressive frescoes depicting key events of the Knights' history painted in 1576 by the Italian Matteo Perez D'Aleccio. Only the State Dining Room holds reminders of the British period, in the form of several royal portraits ranging from George III's to Elizabeth II's time. On a different note, the Council Room (where the ruling council, akin to today's government cabinet, held its meetings) is adorned with copies of the fantastic Gobelin Tapestries, depicting romanticized scenes of New World animals and hunters encountered by the German Prince Johan Mauritz of Nassau during his expedition from 1636 to 1644.

The absorbing **Armoury** (daily 9am–5pm; €4.70) spreads over two barrel-vaulted halls that were used as the palace stables. The Knights had enough military hardware to equip an army of 18,000, and although only a fraction of this haul remains, the 5000 or so pieces on display comprise virtually the whole range of armaments produced between the sixteenth and the eighteenth centuries in Malta and other European countries. An audioguide, included in the entry fee, provides an insightful account of the range of militaria, which also includes the priceless damascened suit of body armour that belonged to Grand Master Wignacourt.

St Paul's Shipwreck Church

Triq San Pawl, Valletta ☎21/236013. Daily: May–Oct 6.30am–noon & 1–7pm; Nov–April 6.30am–7pm. Free. The capital's most impressive church after the Co-Cathedral – the present structure, consecrated in 1740, is the third incarnation on this site – St Paul's is dedicated to the shipwreck of Malta's favourite saint in 60 AD (see p.55). Among its rich and dense interior – which includes silver chandeliers and statues of the Apostles, ornate altars in the side-chapels and a statue of the Archangel trampling over Lucifer – are the memorials to St Paul. These range from a fragment of the saint's wrist bone set in a gilded reliquary and the pillar on which he was beheaded to more creative art works, such as the large painting in the chancel, produced by Matteo Perez D'Aleccio in 1579 for the original church, depicting in dark solemn tones the bishop kneeling in front of St Paul, and a strikingly triumphal statue of St Paul in which the Maltese sculptor Melchiorre Gafa, who produced it aged 22 in 1658, portrays the saint as full of religious rage, with a deep frown and fiery eyes.

Siege Bell Monument

Triq Il-Mediterran, Valletta. Daily 9am–5pm. This huge bell, mounted on a specially built podium, was erected in 1992 and jointly inaugurated by the then Maltese President Ċensu Tabone and Queen Elizabeth II to commemorate the anniversary of the George Cross Award to Malta (see p.56), and to honour the 7000 servicemen and women and civilians that died here during World War II. The bell tolls daily at noon, and its boom can be heard throughout Valletta – intended as a reminder of Malta's war victims.

▲ FORT ST ELMO

Fort St Elmo

St Elmo Place ☎21/237747. St Elmo was built by the Knights in six months during 1552 in preparation for an imminent invasion by the Turks. Its star shape was intended to provide a defence umbrella of crossfire, and the design certainly worked – St Elmo withstood four weeks of cannon fire from three sides before being captured in the first thrust of the Great Siege of 1565. Later, when Valletta was built, the fort was incorporated within the city's fortifications, and during World War II it was hit by a bomb that caused the war's first six casualties. Today, St Elmo houses the police academy, and while the public aren't allowed inside, you can take in its battlemented walls from the square outside the main gate. The doors do open on selected Sundays (1–3 times monthly; €4.66) at 11am for forty-minute re-enactments of a Knights' military parade; the pageantry, which includes ceremonial cannon and musket fire, is colourful in its own right, but it is also an opportunity to see the fort. For specific dates, check the calendar of events at Ⓦwww.visitmalta.com or pick up a brochure from a tourist office.

War Museum

St Sebastian's Spur, Fort St Elmo complex, Valletta ☎21/222430, Ⓦwww.heritagemalta.org. Daily 9am–5pm. €2.33. A range of absorbing exhibits are packed into this small museum dedicated to Malta's role in World War II. The displays range from rank insignias and uniforms to all manner of guns and period photographs showing the ravages of aerial bombardments. Highlights include an Italian speed boat, which was an explosive-packed suicide boat commandeered by the Allies during the invasion of Sicily, but the star exhibit is the aptly named *Faith*, the sole survivor of the three Gloucester Gladiator biplanes that performed so bravely in Malta's air defences in 1939. A copy of the 1942 George Cross award, given to Malta for its endurance during the intense aerial bombing campaign and blockade that pushed the island to the brink of surrender, is also prominently displayed.

Il-Mandraġġ

Occupying the northern corner of Valletta, the crumbling former slum district of Il-Mandraġġ is demarcated on two sides by the sea, and on the other two by Triq It-Teatru L-Antik and Triq Id-Dejqa. Until the 1960s, the area's alleys were alive with the activity of blacksmiths and bakers, and, along Triq Id-Dejqa, a glut of sleazy bars (one or two of which survive), where prostitutes served

British sailors. Squalid and overpopulated, Il-Mandraġġ was described in the 1930s by British writer Evelyn Waugh as "the most concentrated and intense slum in the world". Today, the crumbling stone buildings towering over dank alleys remain faithful to the original urban fabric of Valletta, and it's worth exploring a little to absorb the atmosphere of what's now a safe, if rather desolate, district. Triq Il-Punent cuts through the heart of Il-Mandraġġ, and opens into a small square where a monument commemorates the late-eighteenth-century cleric Mikiel Xerri, leader of a planned coup against the French occupation, who was caught before the plot was enacted and publicly shot along with 34 other cohorts in Misraħ San Ġorġ in 1799. On the west side of the square is the prominently spired Anglican Cathedral of 1839, whose construction was paid for by Queen Adelaide (widow of King William IV) who, when convalescing in Malta, was shocked at the absence of an Anglican church.

Our Lady of Mount Carmel Church

Triq It-Teatru L-Antik, Il-Mandraġġ, Valletta. Daily 7am–9pm. Free.
Following its destruction in World War II, the rebuilding of Our Lady of Mount Carmel (the original dated from the 1570s) took twenty years and demonstrated a reassertion of the dominance of Baroque architecture in Malta. The resulting structure shows more concern with size than it does with artistic detail – the idea seems to have been to make Carmel's egg-shaped dome eclipse the spire of the nearby Anglican Cathedral, but together, the two form a classic feature of Valletta's skyline. The interior is unusually bare by Maltese standards, but is worth a peek to gape at the dizzying hollowness within.

Manoel Theatre

Triq It-Teatru L-Antik, Il-Mandraġġ, Valletta ⓣ21/246389, ⓦwww.teatrumanoel.com.mt. Mon–Fri 10.15am–3.30pm, Sat 10.15am–12.30pm. Tours every 45 minutes. €3.95. Personally funded by Grand Master Antonio

▼ PJAZZA SAN PUBLIJU, FLORIANA

▲ PORTES DES BOMBES

Manoel de Vilhena in 1731, Malta's national theatre is one of Europe's oldest and most impressive. Wholly built from timber, the intimate six-hundred-seat oval-shaped interior is ringed by boxes, some finished in gold. Two reservoirs underground perfect the acoustics, which are so precise that orchestral conductors have to work from one side of the stage to prevent the rustle made by turning the pages of music sheets being audible in the auditorium. The obligatory half-hour guided tours outline the construction of the theatre and its history, but the Manoel is best appreciated during an evening performance (see p.171).

Floriana

Ringed by tiered fortifications, Floriana is a town that was created as – and still feels like – a suburb of Valletta. Although its grid of residential homes hold little allure, it's worth a quick walk down Triq Sarria, the main road leading out of Valletta's bus station, to have a look at the monuments scattered around the district's massive town square,

The Floriana Lines

In the 1630s, as the Turks expanded their fleet, the Knights feared an attack and so commissioned Pietro Paolo Floriani, engineer to the pope, to assess Malta's defences. Floriani proposed a line of fortifications across the neck of the Sciberras Peninsula – enclosing Valletta and in effect creating a new fortified suburb, Floriana – so that Malta's entire population could be crammed behind the defences in the event of an invasion. Critics pointed out that these Floriana Lines were too ambitious and too expensive, but nonetheless work began in 1635; by 1650 the fortifications were almost complete, and entirely girdled the new town of Floriana (named after Floriani). In 1670, the defences were strengthened by means of the Floriana Hornwork, a horn-shaped bulwark jutting out from the Lines' southwest corner, with a fire-range extending across the inner creeks of the Grand Harbour. The Floriana Hornwork and Portes Des Bombes, the sole gate through the fortifications, were completed in 1716 and proved the ultimate deterrent: the Turks never attacked, principally because of the virtual impossibility of breaking through the impenetrable fortifications.

Pjazza San Publiju – particularly the striking golden eagle atop a pillar, commemorating RAF victims of World War II, and the Independence Monument, an ecstatic hands-raised woman who seems to levitate with the symbolic euphoria of freedom – and then continue to Argotti and St Philip Gardens.

Underneath Pjazza San Publiju are a series of underground chambers that were dug out by the Knights to store enough grain for two years in the event of an invasion and blockade; the stone caps of the now-sealed chambers are raised above the surface of the square, which is dominated by the mammoth church of San Publiju, a monumental setpiece whose interior – largely dim and comparatively bare – is anti-climactic.

Less than 100m further down the road, **Argotti Garden** (daily 7.30am–dusk; free) was originally the private garden of a knight before being converted into a botanical garden in 1805 – an ambitious claim for what remains a small and incomplete collection of exotic plants and trees. The main draw here, however, is the view of Floriana's fortifications which zigzag in both directions from the edge of the garden.

There's an even better perspective of the walls from the neighbouring **St Philip Garden** (daily 7.30am–1pm; free), which is set around and on a ravelin – a triangular bastion set apart from the main wall as a forward gun emplacement. The ravelin is now smothered in a profusion of citrus groves, climbing vines, cypresses, palms and cacti, and it also holds the Wignacourt Fountain, a High Baroque affair built by the Knights to commemorate the completion of the aqueduct that channeled spring water, by gravity, from the heights of Rabat to Valletta. The fountain was erected in Misraħ San Ġorġ and then eventually dismantled and moved to St Philip Garden.

Hotels

British

40 Triq Il-Batterija, Valletta ⓣ21/224730, ⓦwww.britishhotel.com. One of Malta's oldest hotels is set in a large townhouse that holds eight en-suite rooms kitted out with pine furniture, funky lampshades and landscape paintings. Best are the airy and spacious superior rooms overlooking the Grand Harbour, which cost €70; smaller standard twin rooms are €24. Mobile a/c €7 extra.

Grand Harbour

47 Triq Il-Batterija, Valletta ⓣ21/246003, ⓦwww.grandharbourhotel.com. Budget base, with cramped corridors and staircases, but the rooms have recently been renovated with new furniture and TVs,

▼ TRIQ IR-REBUBBLIKA

▲ GOLD SHOP

and most of them have a/c and bathrooms. Rooms on the front have excellent views of the Grand Harbour. Doubles from €50, breakfast included.

Osborne

50 Triq Nofs In-Nhar, Valletta ⓣ21/243656, ⓦwww.osbornehotel.com. A distinctly old-world atmosphere in the lobby and adjoining restaurant gives way to 59 large, stylishly furnished en-suite rooms, with a/c, phone and TV – although, pitifully, many of the rooms have no windows. Doubles from €60.

Phoenicia

Vjal Ir-Re Dwardu VII, Floriana ⓣ21/225241, ⓦwww.phoeniciamalta.com. The area's best hotel, situated next to the bus station, has traditionally decorated rooms with tiled floors, flower-themed curtains and good amenities – including Internet – but bland white-tiled bathrooms. Common facilities are extensive, and the French restaurant is excellent. Doubles from €163, breakfast included.

Hostel

Dar Niki Cassar

178 Triq Il-Merkanti, Valletta ⓣ21/240680, ⓔinfo@ymcahomeless.org. Malta's best-value hostel, set in a historic four-storey townhouse with beautiful floor tiles, airy and cool six-bed dorms, a great view from the roof and friendly management. Facilities include Internet access, washing machines and a large kitchen. Dorm beds €7, breakfast included.

Shops

Anthony Preca

157 Triq Santa Luċija, Valletta ⓣ21/221165. Mon–Fri 8.45am–12.30pm & 4–7pm, Sat 8.45am–12.30pm. The oldest and most reliable of the gold shops along this stretch, offering an exciting assortment of traditional designs, including Maltese crosses.

Meli Bookshop

185 Triq Il-Fran, Valletta ⓣ21/237266. Mon–Fri 9am–1pm & 4–7pm, Sat 9am–1pm. A good selection of English-language titles in all genres – including reference, guidebooks, novels and travel. Many are remaindered stock, and sell for half the published price, but there are new titles too.

Sapienza's Bookshop

Triq Ir-Repubblika, Valletta ⓣ21/233621. Mon–Fri 9am–7pm, Sat 9am–1pm. Valletta's largest bookshop, with a good selection of Malta-related titles as well as reference, classics and fiction.

Saulus

282a Triq San Pawl, Valletta ⓣ79430027 (mobile). Mon–Fri 10.30am–12.30pm & 4.45–7pm, Sat 9.30am–12.30pm. A large range of Catholic icons and other religious artefacts, ranging from tiny chalices and crosses to metre-high china Madonnas. Look out for *pasturi* – finger-sized clay figurines depicting traditional Maltese characters in period dress that can make nice ornaments.

Cafés

Café Jubilee

125 Triq Santa Luċija, Valletta ☎21/252332. Daily 8am–1am; closed Aug. Cosy place serving great coffee, pasta dishes, large *pastizzi* and other snacks. Very busy and raucous during winter lunchtimes, but quieter in summer when the Maltese vacate Valletta for the beaches. The flock-wallpapered walls are a kaleidoscope of curio prints, and the music is tasteful, ranging from world to classical music and ambient techno.

Chiaroscuro

44 Triq Id-Dejqa, Valletta ☎21/228250. Mon–Sat 9am–11pm. This large old townhouse's various rooms spread over two floors make a rich setting for a café, which serves Malta's best coffees as well as food all day – ranging from creative, Italian one-plate meals to a buffet of Italian antipasti and some hot dishes (served 11.30am–3.30pm). In the evenings it morphs into a wine bar and on Fridays and Saturdays, when it's open later, there's live jazz.

Restaurants

Ambrosia

137 Triq L-Arċisqof, Valletta ☎21/225923. Mon 12.30–2pm, Tues–Sat 12.30–2pm & 7.30–10pm. Closed two weeks in Sept and the first week of Jan. Cooked by one of Malta's most celebrated chefs and served in an informal room with warm auburn walls, the daily changing menu of pastas, salads, meats and fish includes favourites such as goat's cheese soufflé, tuna carpaccio, fettuccini with ricotta and rocket or chicken liver and fig salad, for €7–16 per dish.

The Carriage

22/5 Valletta Buildings, Triq Nofs In-Nhar, Valletta ☎21/247828. Mon–Fri noon–3.30pm, plus Fri & Sat 7.30–11.30pm. Closed two weeks in Aug. Neat, neutrally decorated place that attracts upscale business-people for lunch. The service is professional and the cooking creative – you might

▼ PASTURI STATUETTES

start with breaded aubergine stuffed with mozzarella, or spinach and mascarpone ravioli with basil and pine nuts; main courses include steamed grouper with oyster mushrooms and ginger, and roast quail stuffed with aubergines and sage. Main courses around €16, and there's a three-course set menu for €20.

The Circle's Café

141 Messina Palace, St Christopher St, Valletta ☎21/244863. Mon–Fri 7am–6pm, Sat 7am–2pm. Informal café in a covered courtyard serving up large portions of pasta from a daily changing menu. Fillings for *ftira* rolls include the traditional tuna, olive oil, pickled vegetables and tomato paste. Service is instant, and prices a bargain – under €5 for pastas, and under €2.50 for *ftiras*.

Malata

Misraħ San Ġorġ, Valletta ☎21/233967. Mon–Sat noon–3pm & 7–11pm. One of Malta's best restaurants, with seating in an atmospheric cellar or at outdoor tables facing the Grand Master's Palace. The menu changes seasonally and adventurous mains (around €17) include the excellent quails stuffed with foie gras and cooked in port wine. There's live jazz on Tuesday and Friday.

Papanni's

55 Triq Id-Dejqa, Valletta ☎21/251960. Mon–Sat noon–2.30pm & 7–10pm. Italian-style trattoria set within the honey-coloured stone walls of a converted townhouse, offering standard antipasti, pastas, risotto, salads, grilled meats and fish at moderate prices.

Da Pippo

136 Triq Melita, Valletta ☎21/248029. Mon–Sat noon–3.30pm. Small, informal Italian-style trattoria that's good for quick lunches. Daily specials and Maltese staples include stuffed marrows, *bragioli* (steak stuffed with minced pork), and grilled fish with salad and roast potatoes. The handsome antipasti is on the house and includes local delicacies such as *bigilla* (broad-bean dip) and *ġbejniet* (Gozitan cheese). About €13 for main courses.

Rubino

53 Triq Il-Fran, Valletta ☎21/224656. Mon–Fri 12.15–2.30pm, plus Tues & Fri 7.45–10.30pm. Closed Aug. The best place on the island for modestly priced but well-executed Maltese-based

▼ THE CARRIAGE RESTAURANT

▲ MAESTRO E'FRESCO

cuisine. The menu is changed every few days, and recurrent seasonal dishes include pasta with minced pork, white wine and bay leaves; tuna with balsamic vinegar, mint and green peppercorns; Maltese-style sautéed meat-balls; and the dessert Cassata Siciliana, a lovely Italian cake. Tuesday evenings are dedicated to rabbit cooked in garlic, white wine, bay leaf and rosemary (a giveaway at €11.75).

Sicilia

1A Triq San Ġwann, Valletta ☎21/240569. Tues–Sat noon–2.30pm. Popular, brisk and inexpensive lunch spot serving generous portions of Sicilian-style pasta, meat and fish dishes, plus a selection of Maltese snacks, including *ftira*. Seating is on an outdoor terrace with views of the Grand Harbour.

Bars

Maestro E'Fresco

8 Triq Nofs In-Nhar, Valletta. ☎21/220357. Daily 10am–midnight. Café-bar and live-music venue, where the white decor – white walls, couches and stools – contrasts stylishly with teak furnishings. The music mostly consists of chill-out lounge tunes, and on Friday and Saturday at 9pm live bands roll out light rock.

Q Bar

Vault 1, Waterfront, Valletta ☎21/223018. Daily 6pm–2am. The most creative and funkiest bar among a dozen varied outlets on the Waterfront, the newly restored sea passenger terminal in the Grand Harbour. You can sit outdoors and enjoy a bottle of wine and finger food such as a Maltese-style platter or sushi, or go indoors to a Knights-era warehouse to join a thirty-something crowd in a lounge-club where occasional live bands play jazz or soul, or a DJ spins chilled dance tunes.

Trabuxu

Triq Id-Dejqa, Valletta ☎21/223036. Tues–Sun 7pm–1am. Wine bar set in an atmospheric old cellar that attracts a laidback Maltese crowd for the good selection of 260 wines. Prices start from a modest €10 for a mid-range Maltese Cabernet Sauvignon, and you can tuck into one of the various platters, or the always popular cheese fondue, while jazz and blues music flutters in the background.

The Three Cities

Occupying two narrow peninsulas on the other side of the Grand Harbour from Valletta and enclosed on the land side by Malta's largest defensive fortification, the Three Cities of Vittoriosa, Senglea and Cospicua retain a romantic, medieval urban fabric that makes them a pleasure to wander through, with a scattering of individual sights on which to focus your exploration. Malta's second-oldest town, atmospheric Vittoriosa (sometimes known by its old name, Birgu) has the highest concentration of individual attractions; both Senglea and Cospicua, which sustained heavy damage during World War II, have less to recommend them, though Senglea offers great views from a garden at the tip of the peninsula. It's also worth travelling east of the Three Cities to see the gigantic cannon at Fort Rinella.

The Three Gates and Malta At War Museum

Triq Boffa, Vittoriosa. Until the Three Cities' fortifications were breached for vehicular access, the grandiose, three-tiered Three Gates provided the sole entrance to Vittoriosa. The first, the exuberantly Baroque **Advanced Gate**, was built in 1722, and opens into an elegantly restored courtyard from where a network of claustrophobic tunnels and small rooms were gouged into the bedrock to serve as the town's shelter during World War II. Now an excellent **museum** (daily 10am–4pm; €4.66; ⓣ21/896617, ⓦwww.wirtartna.org) to that era, the place holds an array of original artefacts such as gas masks, sirens, pickaxes and guns, and period re-creations of the rooms as they would have been when occupied during the war, including bedrooms, a chapel and a clinic. A visit starts with a documentary about Malta's war experience, and then a guided tour of the complex itself

Visiting the Three Cities

Buses #1 and #2 from Valletta, and #627 from Sliema and Buġibba, go past Senglea and through Cospicua, and call at Vittoriosa's small bus terminus outside the town walls. Bus #4, which also departs from Valletta, calls at Vittoriosa's terminus and continues to Kalkara and Fort Rinella. There's plenty of parking throughout the Three Cities, especially along the waterfront and in the town squares. You can get a great perspective of the Three Cities from the Grand Harbour's waters; informal tours aboard wooden boats known as *kajjik* depart from the harbourside in front of Vittoria's St Lawrence Church (daily 9am–8pm) and cost around €12 per boat for half an hour. The *kajjiks* can also drop you off in Valletta, near the Customs House, for €4.66 for a single commuter or €2.33 each for more sharing; or in Sliema for €6 per person (though this service is suspended during blustery conditions).

which also has two colourful animatronic displays: men digging shelters with pickaxes, and a re-creation of an aerial bombardment raid as would have been experienced by the inhabitants cowering within.

Continuing north past the museum takes you over a bridge spanning the dry moat between two sets of fortifications, and through the **Couvre Porte Gate**, the second of the three, which opens into a bare stone courtyard from which worn-out stairs head up to the ramparts; at the top you get a good view of the complex fortifications. Across this courtyard is the third **Main Gate**, on the other side of which is Triq Il-Mina L-Kbira, the main road leading into Vittoriosa.

The Inquisitors' Palace

Triq Il-Mina Il-Kbira, Vittoriosa ⓣ21/827006, ⓦwww.heritagemalta.org. Daily 9am–5pm. €4.66. Built as law courts in the thirteenth century, this large Baroque building became the seat for Malta's Inquisition between 1574 and 1798. The present two-storey structure was remodelled and enlarged following damage from an earthquake in 1693, and it now makes a fascinating place to explore. The highlight of the **ground floor** is the beautiful central courtyard, with ribbed cross-vaults, built by the Knights soon after their arrival in Malta in 1530. At the rear of the ground floor you can peek into the building's musty, bare prison cells, whose only feature is a small high window providing natural light; internees' anguished graffiti is still visible on the walls.

▲ MAIN GATE, VITTORIOSA

▼ VITTORIOSA SQUARE

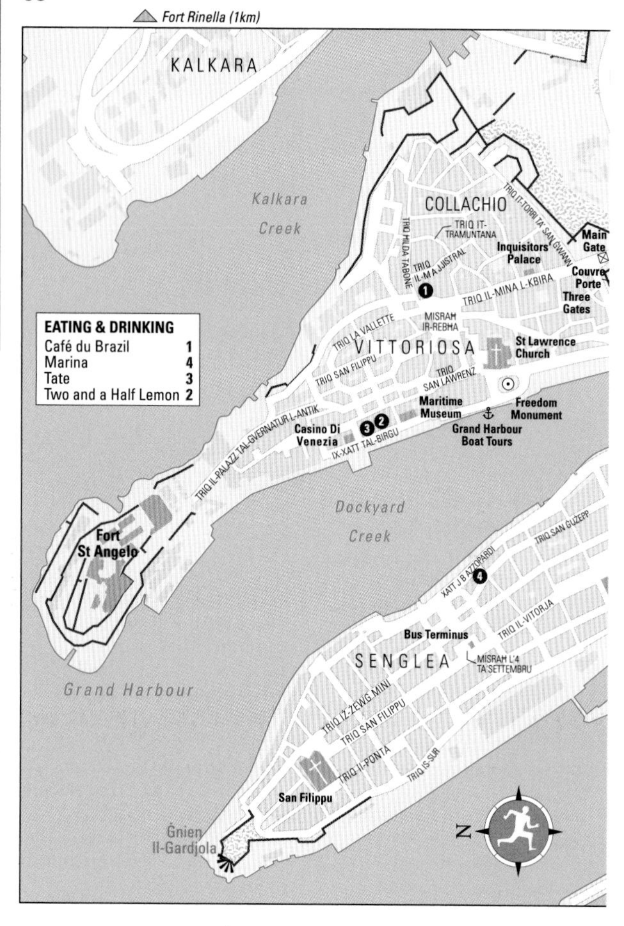

The sombre **upper floor**, reached via a pompous Baroque staircase, was the public domain of the Inquisitor. The largest room is the Chancery, with a worn wooden ceiling and walls holding the dull coats of arms of Malta's 63 Inquisitors. This connects to the Waiting Room, where visitors had to wait for an audience with the Inquisitor in a space of garish faded-blue walls topped by a frieze of Baroque stone scrolls. There's an almost tangible feel of desolation both here and in the adjacent Audience Hall, where the Inquisitor entertained guests, a mood not lightened by the pink walls and Baroque friezes. Yet the highlight of the upper floor is the austere Tribunal Room next door, where the intimidating Inquisitor's throne contrasts with the low stool on which the accused sat. Behind is a half-sized door, designed to force even the most intransigent of prisoners to bow to the Inquisitor.

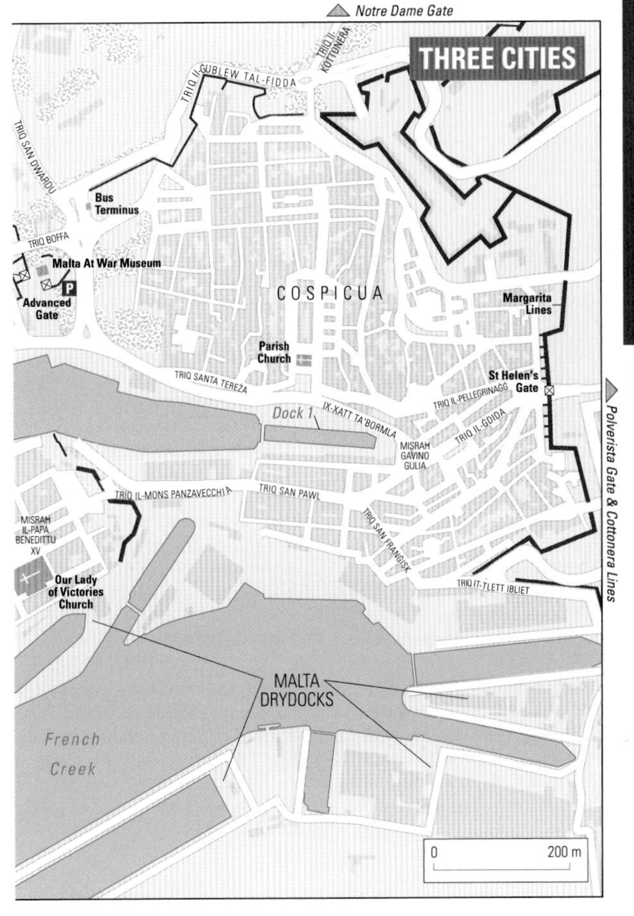

The Collachio

Vittoriosa. Home-base of the Knights between 1530 and 1571, this ancient quarter is the most attractive part of Vittoriosa. Characterized by winding pedestrianized alleys full of potted plants and restored buildings, it's a perfect place to lose yourself on a warm afternoon. The Knights' Baroque townhouses or *auberges* survive along Triq Ħilda Tabone and Triq Il-Majjistral; all have been converted, with few alterations, into public buildings or private residences.

St Lawrence Church

Xatt Ir-Risq, Vittoriosa. Daily 6–9.30am & 4–6pm. Free.

St Lawrence Church sits evocatively atop a high parapet on the town's western shore, which amplifies its size and grand setting. The original building was one of Malta's earliest medieval parish churches, said to have been constructed by Roger the

▲ ST LAWRENCE CHURCH

Norman after he snatched Malta from Arab rule in 1090, and it served as the Knights' conventual church between 1530 and 1571. The present structure dates from 1681, and was the first of a spate of triumphal churches designed by master Maltese architect Lorenzo Gafa, who shunned the fad for ornate Baroque during his time, and instead created a grand presence with the architectural setting and composition. The highlight of the otherwise gloomy interior is the altarpiece by Mattia Preti – his largest ever painting, it's a tense depiction of the martyrdom of St Lawrence, infused with dark suspense.

Malta Maritime Museum

Ix-Xatt Tal-Birgu, Vittoriosa ⓣ21/660052, ⓦwww.heritagemalta.org. Daily 9am–5pm. €4.66. Situated in the British-built former naval bakery, the Maritime Museum holds an interesting collection pertaining to Malta's illustrious seafaring history. Exhibits on the upper floor are grouped by era, starting with the British section, which consists mainly of photographs and models of ships alongside some compasses – fantastic and complicated contraptions that aided early navigation. The largest hall is dedicated to the Knights' naval history, with cannons, paintings of famous sea battles and various models of Knightly boats, ranging from the ceremonial vessels of the Grand Masters to a large model of a standard eighteenth-century military galley, the museum's star exhibit. It was with these robust ships that the Knights commanded the seas in the central Mediterranean – the Spanish are said to have recognized the severest of storms as the ones "which only the galleys of Malta could weather".

Fort St Angelo

Ix-Xatt Tal-Birgu, Vittoriosa. This large stronghold stands as a highly impressive monument to, and symbol of, Malta's militaristic past, but unfortunately it lies in a state of neglect and you can only appreciate it from outside its walls as it's not currently open to the public. St Angelo, which has existed since 1200 at the latest (no one knows for sure when it was built), has withstood all of Malta's major historical battles. It served as the first Maltese base of the Knights, who enlarged it and strengthened the fortifications, so ensuring that its defences weren't penetrated by the Turks during the Great Siege of 1565. Following the arrival of the British, it passed to the Royal Navy and, with a ship's mast placed on top to make it look the part, became the HMS St Angelo, the Navy's shore establishment. The 69 World War II bombs that hit caused only superficial damage, and it remained in military use until the British forces left Malta in 1979.

Since then, three decades of governmental incompetence and indifference have left the fort in a dishevelled state, its walls starting to crack. Discussions about the fort's restoration have been ongoing for many years now – and remain entangled in the divergent agendas of all the groups who have a legal stake in the fort (the owners of the yacht marina, Heritage Malta, Wirt Artna, and the Knights themselves who occupy its upper reaches). In the meantime, you can admire the fort from outside, and the best views of it are from Ġnien Il-Gardjola (see p.70)

Senglea

Senglea was founded by Knights in the 1550s and takes its name from Claude de la Sengle, Grand Master at the time. The nascent town was severely damaged in the Great Siege of 1565, and 400 years later it was almost completely razed again during World War II. The town's parish church, **Our Ladies of Victories Church** in the main square, Misraħ Papa Benedittu XV (daily 6–11am & 4–6.45pm; free), named to commemorate the Knights' conquest in the Great Siege, is an imposing edifice that was completely rebuilt after it was obliterated during World War II to clear the way for German aircraft to dive-bomb

The Cottonera Lines and Notre Dame Gate

Cospicua, a derivative of "conspicuous", is so-called because the town lay outside Vittoriosa's fortifications during the Great Siege, and so was razed to the ground. It was subsequently rebuilt, and protected by an arc of fortifications that encircled the Three Cities at the landward side, called the Margarita Lines. Eventually, advances in military technology and the modernization of the Ottoman striking armada rendered the Margarita Lines ineffective – an enemy situated on the hillocks outside the wall could lob cannon shells into the Three Cities – and this led to the conception of a second-tier wall beyond the Margarita Lines, called the Cottonera Lines. The plan was criticized by many military engineers as being too ambitious in scale and for maintaining regular height over an irregular terrain of hillocks. However, work on the wall started in the 1670s and took some fifty years to finish: the Cottonera Lines, wholly intact to this day, is a heavy semi-circular wall that envelops the Three Cities at their land front. It is studded with eight triangular bastions – to facilitate a 260-degree sweep of fire – and two demi-bastions where it connects with the fortifications of Senglea and Vittoriosa.

There were seven gates along the Lines, the most sumptuous being the **Notre Dame Gate**, which has been restored by the historic trust Wirt Artna and is now open as a museum (Triq Il-Kottonera, just over 1km east from Vittoriosa's bus station; daily 10am–5pm; €2.33; ⓣ21/803091; ⓦwww.wirtartna.org). The gate, built between 1707 and 1715, is a massive structure that holds bombproof chambers which served as barracks and ammunition stores; it's also a highly ornate Baroque edifice that's adorned by a large coat of arms which holds, amid dense carvings of leafy and triumphant symbols, a bust of Grand Master Nicola Cotoner, who initiated the Cottonera Lines that were named after him. A visit starts with a guided tour, a documentary about the history of the Cottonera Lines, and the chance to go up to the roof and enjoy sweeping views of the Three Cities and beyond. The restoration is ongoing – the plan is to re-create the original ditch or dry moat, and rebuild the bridge.

Malta's dockyards. Its bald, architecturally uninspiring facade with embedded columns prefaces a sumptuous interior, with blood-red velvet curtains and a massive altar, but the church is best known for its statue of *Kristu Redentur*, which attracts a constant trickle of believers for its alleged miraculous healing powers. A moving depiction of a bloodied Christ collapsing on all fours under the burden of the cross, the statue resides in a chapel reached through a doorway to the right of the altar.

Running north from the church square, the town's main road, Triq Il-Vitorja, stretches almost all the way to the tip of the peninsula, passing handsome Baroque townhouses and, towards the end where it connects with Triq San Filippu, an older area that survived the war. Continuing north, via Triq Il-Ponta, brings you to the gate of **Ġnien Il-Gardjola** (daily 7am–dusk; free), a small garden with a sentry post (on which the carvings, an eye and an ear, were meant as a warning that the Knights had eyes and ears everywhere). The garden offers the best views of the Grand Harbour and Fort St Angelo, and down on the Senglea shore on Dockyard Creek, reachable through alleyways from the garden, you get the best views of Vittoriosa. The kiosk on the promenade that skirts the waterline offers overpriced refreshments.

Fort Rinella

Triq Santu Rokku, Kalkara ⓣ21/809713, ⓦwww.wirtartna.org. Daily 9am–5pm. €7. Bus #4 from Valletta, via Vittoriosa bus terminus, then a signposted 10min walk. North of the Three Cities in the town of Kalkara, Fort Rinella was erected by the British in the 1870s specifically to operate the Armstrong 100-ton gun. The largest cannon ever made, it was designed so that its shells could pierce the steel plates of ships as far as three miles away, and hence protect the sea routes leading to the Grand Harbour; it was fired just forty times, the last time in 1905, but it's unclear from historical records whether it actually hit anything. The fort itself is a one of Malta's few examples of Victorian military architecture, and has been sensitively restored by Wirt Artna. Period furnishings and decor have been re-created, and you can study the intricate machinery that operated the Armstrong – the gun is so heavy that it needed a mini coal-fired power station to turn its barrel for aiming. Excellent hourly demonstrations on various subjects, such as food preparation in the fort, evoke

▼ SENGLEA

▲ THE KNIGHTS' FORMER NAVY HEADQUARTERS, VITTORIOSA WATERFRONT, NOW A CASINO

life here during its heyday, or you can opt to visit for the daily historical re-enactments at 2.30pm (€12 entry at this time) with hour-long shows during which "soldiers" offer an animated guided tour, and do a military drill, firing cannon and musket blanks, inviting visitors to participate.

Cafés

Café du Brazil

1 Misraħ Ir-Rebħa, Vittoriosa ☎79295718. Daily 8am–6pm. Set in a corner of the town square, with indoor and outdoor seating, this place serves inexpensive coffees and drinks, as well as snacks such as filled rolls, English breakfasts and lunchtime pasta dishes.

Tate

Ix-Xatt Tal-Birgu, Vittoriosa ☎21/808828. Daily 10am–11.30pm. The funkiest of a scattering of new cafés along the Vittoriosa waterfront, with handsome wooden furniture, set inside a historic vault, and more tables outside on the promenade. It's also Malta's only dedicated vegetarian restaurant, serving an array of interesting snacks for €5 to €10.

Restaurants

Marina

12 Xatt J.B. Azzopard, Senglea ☎21/664398. June–Sept daily 6.30–11pm; Oct–May Mon & Wed–Sun 6.30–10.30pm. This small, pleasant restaurant on Senglea's shore affords great views of Vittoriosa, and cooks up hearty Italian food – there's a range of pasta dishes for €5.50 to €9, fish or meat at between €10 and €14 and pizzas for €5.

Two and a Half Lemon

Ix-Xatt Tal-Birgu, Vittoriosa ☎21/809909. Daily 12.30–3.30pm & 7.30–11pm (closed Sun lunch); Oct–May closed Tues. Vittoriosa's best restaurant – in a tasteful yellow-themed vault and with outdoor tables on the waterfront's promenade – is famous for its lava rock grill (around €17.50): various meats, including kangaroo, are placed on a heated lava rock to grill slowly at the table in front of diners. It also offers much more on a menu full of creative dishes (around €13) of meat, fish and pasta.

Sliema and St Julian's

Sprawled along the coast for some 4km, Sliema and St Julian's together comprise Malta's most cosmopolitan urban centre. These relatively young towns emerged as the island's foremost entertainment and nightlife centres in the 1980s; in the 1990s a string of luxury hotels and condominiums pushed the area further upscale, though the odd inexpensive guesthouse remains. These facilities pull in the tourists, and despite the dearth of historical sights, the good transport connections make the area a convenient base to strike out from, while remaining close to the nightlife scene.

Triq It-Torri (Tower Road)

Sliema. Starting at Sliema Ferries, cutting across the Tigne Peninsula and skirting the coast all the way to Balluta Bay in St Julian's, Triq It-Torri (more commonly known as Tower Road) sees most of Sliema's action. Hemmed in by high-rises on the land side, its wide, attractive promenade on the sea side is Malta's most popular spot for *passiġġata*, with locals and visitors ambling along enjoying the evening air or pausing for an ice cream or *imqaret* (deep-fried date pastry) and a soft drink in summer. The rocky belt sandwiched between the road and the sea serves as a de facto "beach", with ladders allowing access into the sea. Teenage English-language students congregate around Ferro Bay, while local families tend to occupy the hundred-metre stretch on either side of

Visiting Sliema and St Julian's

Buses to and from all the island's resorts and from Valletta (p.47) call at the small, tourist-oriented bus station at Sliema ferries, as do commuter boats that depart from Valletta's Il-Mandraġġ district. If you happen to be around when boats from Vittoriosa (see p.64) drop off passengers, you can get a ride on their return journey to Vittoriosa. There's another small bus terminus on the outskirts of Paċeville, which serves the nightlife district. Late buses from Valletta run here during the week until 1.30am (later on weekends and summer); on Fridays and Saturdays, there are also services to Buġibba (#49), and on Saturday the services are extended to Vittoriosa (#18) and Rabat (#81).

It's difficult to find a parking spot in Sliema and St Julian's congested streets, so if you're driving, your best bet is the multi-storey car park on High Street in Sliema's shopping zone, or the expensive car park at Portomaso in St Julian's.

For taxis, try the 24hr Wembley's Garage on Triq San Ġorġ (☎21/374141 or ☎21/374242); on winter weekends and on most nights in the summer, Wembley's also offer shared taxis (or minibuses if customer volume demands) to any given destination.

▲ SUNBATHERS, EXILES

the Surfside private lido, where you pay a small fee to rent a sun lounger and use the showers. Below the next bend in Tower Road, near the Peace Garden with flowerbeds, fountains and a playground, the area known as Exiles draws Malta's yuppies.

Balluta Bay

St Julian's. Sliema slides imperceptibly into St Julian's at Balluta Bay, with its quiet coastal street leading on to a small triangular piazza, Misraħ Il-Balluta, peppered with Judas trees, benches and outdoor seating for a handful of mediocre restaurants. Although there's no swimming to be had in the shallow, silty water which laps against the promenade's concrete embankment, the piazza is a pleasant, sunny spot, with a few cafés that make a nice place for an afternoon drink. The square's eastern flank is dominated by the monumental Balluta Buildings, a fantastic 1920s Art Nouveau apartment block whose arches, intricate angel motifs and terraced profile provide an ornate contrast to the other bland high-rises fringing the bay.

Spinola Bay

St Julian's. Lined with apartment blocks and home to legions of restaurants, cafés, bars and hotels, this compact, kidney-shaped bay is always bustling with people strolling along the promenade that skirts the waterline and watching the fishermen mending nets in front of their boathouses. The bay itself remains home to a dwindling number of moored-up *luzzu*, painted in vibrant colours, decorated with Baroque designs and sporting the much-photographed "Eyes of Osiris" on their bows to lead to good fishing grounds. Many of Spinola Bay's restaurants have

▼ SPINOLA BAY

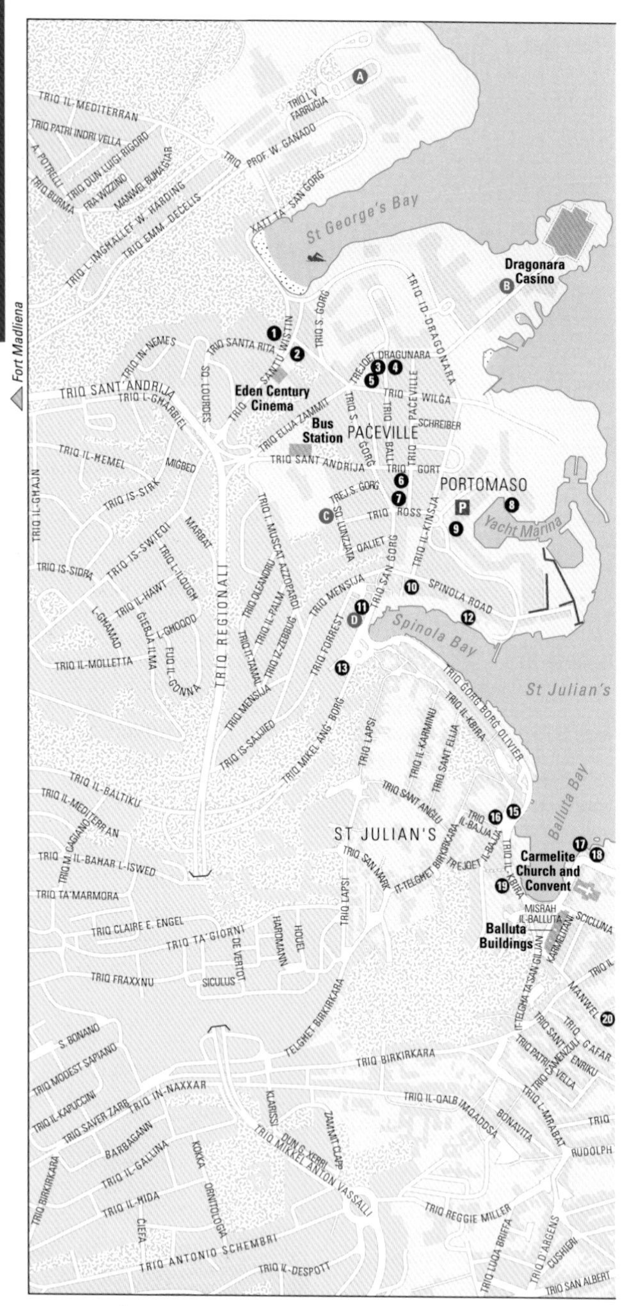
St George's Bay
Dragonara Casino
Eden Century Cinema
Bus Station
PACEVILLE
PORTOMASO
Yacht Marina
Spinola Bay
St Julian's
Balluta Bay
ST JULIAN'S
Carmelite Church and Convent
Balluta Buildings
Fort Madliena
TRIQ SANT ANDRIJA
TRIQ REGIONALI
SPINOLA ROAD
TRIQ BIRKIRKARA
TRIQ MIKIEL ANTON VASSALLI
TRIQ ANTONIO SCHEMBRI
TRIQ IL-MEDITERRAN
TRIQ SAN GORG
TRIQ ID-DRAGONARA
TRIQ IL-KBIRA
MISRAH IL-BALLUTA

SLIEMA & ST JULIAN'S

EATING, DRINKING & NIGHTLIFE

The Avenue	6	Havana	2	Places	3
Barracuda	17	Il-Merill	22	Radisson Bistro	A
BJ's Nightclub and Piano Bar	4	Juuls	10	Ryan's Irish Pub	13
Black Gold	25	The Kitchen	14	The Scotsman Pub	7
Blue Elephant	8	Misto	24	Simon's Pub	20
Café Jubilee	26	Muddy Waters	16	Stella's Coffee Shop	21
City of London	15	Offshore	23	Terrazza	12
Coconut Grove	5	Peppino's	11	Wiġi's Kitchen	19
Fuego	1	Piccolo Padre	18	Żeri's	9
				Zest	D

SHOP

Bread Bakery a

ACCOMMODATION

Comfort Inn	I
Dean Hamlet	C
Fortina	K
Hibernia House	F
Juliani	D
Imperial	H
Radisson SAS Bay Point Resort	A
Victoria	G
The Waterfront	J
Westin Dragonara	B
Windsor	E

N

0 200 m

Bay
EXILES
Peace Promenade Gardens
TRIQ IT-TORRI
WINDSOR TERRACE
TRIQ IL-CRECHE
TRIQ SAN GWANN BOSCO
Surfside Lido
DINGLI CIRCUS
TRIQ IT-TORRI
TRIQ SIR G. BORG
TRIQ SIR ADRIAN DINGLI
TRIQ GUŻE HOWARD
TRIQ DUN MIKIEL RUA
TRIQ SIR ARTURO MERCIECA
CAMILLERI
OLIVIER
FERRO BAY
TRIQ IL-KBIRA
L-ANTIK
TRIQ IN-NAZZARENU
TRIQ SAN FRANĠISK
TRIQ NIKOLO ISOUARD
SANTA MARGARITA
TRIQ NORFOLK
N. POUTIATIN
TRIQ MELITA
TRIQ SIR LUIGI
TRIQ GORG BORG
TRIQ AMERY
L. GRAHAM
LUZZU
TRIQ GUŻE HOWARD
TRIQ MILNER
TRIQ IT-TORRI
Sliema Point Battery
KULLEĠ
SANT IGNAZJU
TRIQ DEPIRO
TRIQ STELLA
TRIQ BLANCHE HUBER
TRIQ SANT ELENA
SLIEMA
GHAR ID-DUD
GHAR ID-DUD
TRIQ IL-KBIRA
N. FALZON
TRIQ RUDOLPH
ANNUNCIATION
TRIQ SAN NIKOLA SQUARE
TRIQ SAN PAWL
HIGH STREET
IX-XATT TA' QUI SI-SANA
DIMECH STREET
SAN KARLU
SANT ALFONSU
TRIQ SAN GWANN BATTISTE
TRIQ IL-KARMNU
TRIQ SANTA MARIJA
TRIQ IL-LUNZJATA
TRIQ IL-KATIDRAL
TONNA
TRIQ SAN TROFIMU
TRIQ SAN VINĊENZ
TRIQ PAPA PIJU V
STREET
Police Station
TRIQ MANWEL DIMECH STREET
TRIQ IT-TORRI
Plaza Shopping Complex
BISAZZA ST
TRIQ G. BENCINI
TRIQ VIANI
SANT AGATA
Bus Terminus
TRIQ MORONI
GZIRA
Ferries to Valletta
TIGNE
SLIEMA FERRIES
TRIQ IX-XATT
TRIQ IX-XATT TA' TIGNE
PJAZZA MEME SCICLUNA
TRIQ SAN ALBERT
Health Centre
Marsamxett Harbour

J (500m), 26, Valletta & Manoel Island

K & Fort Tigne

terraces overlooking the sea, and the bay makes a lovely spot to have dinner, with the lights shimmering romantically on the water.

Paċeville

St Julian's. Paċeville remains Malta's prime nightlife district, with dozens of bars and clubs rubbing shoulders at ground level, and high-rise resort-style apartment blocks towering overhead. Shabby and haphazardly planned, Paċeville is pretty much deserted during the day, but picks up nightly throughout the summer and at weekends in winter when thousands of young people descend on the quarter. It's a boisterous and generally amicable scene – with loud music blaring from the open-fronted bars and people spilling on to the pavements.

Hotels

Fortina

Triq Ix-Xatt Ta' Tigne, Sliema ⓣ23/460000, ⓦwww.hotelfortina.com. Split into two separate buildings (offering four- and five-star accommodation), the *Fortina* has become something of an institution, situated in a good location for transport and Valletta views, just five minutes' walk from Sliema ferries. The five-star section has a rich array of rooms, while the older four-star wing has cosy rooms with all amenities (rooms were slated for a refurbishment at the time of writing). Common facilities include some good Asian restaurants and an impressive spa where treatments include concentrated seawater healing techniques. Doubles from €160 for four-star rooms, and from €260 for the five-star wing.

Imperial

Triq Rudolph, Sliema ⓣ21/344093, ⓦwww.imperialhotelmalta.com. Sizeable Baroque townhouse in the centre of Sliema, with classy touches such as ceiling murals, and an elegant garden framed by stone arches. The interior is quiet and cool, and the pleasant, tidy and spacious rooms have TVs, a/c and phones. Twins from €75, breakfast included.

Juliani

12 Triq San Ġorġ, St Julian's ⓣ21/388000, ⓦwww.hoteljuliani.com. The facade

▼ BAROQUE TOWNHOUSE, ANNUNCIATION SQUARE, SLIEMA

retains the look of a typical Baroque townhouse, but the interior is inspired by modern Asian decor. The 44 double rooms have spacious bathrooms, large beds, TVs, phones and plenty of stylish touches; there's also a great Asian fusion restaurant on site. Doubles from €150.

Radisson SAS Bay Point

Triq L V Farruġia, St George's Bay, St Julian's ⓣ21/374894, ⓦwww.islandhotels.com. The most northerly of the string of upmarket hotels slung around the St Julian's coast, this cream-painted, boomerang-shaped building boasts a grand lobby, several restaurants and pools and a large gym. The spacious, sumptuously decorated open-plan rooms have all mod cons and sea views. Doubles from €190, breakfast included.

Victoria

Triq Ġorġ Borġ Olivier, Sliema ⓣ21/334711, ⓦwww.victoriahotel.com. In the heart of Sliema, ten minutes' walk from the seafront, this cream-coloured tower block has elegant, modern rooms decorated in warm colours and with all mod cons. There's a small pool on the roof. Doubles €140.

Waterfront

Triq Ix-Xatt, Gżira ⓣ21/333434, ⓦwww.waterfronthotelmalta.com. Conveniently situated on the fringes of Sliema, overlooking Manoel Island, this is a modern, functional and comfortable four-star place with good service. The en-suite rooms are tasteful and have a/c, phones and TVs; you pay an extra €12 for a room with a sea view at the front. Doubles €98, breakfast included.

Westin Dragonara

Triq Dragonara, St Julian's ⓣ21/381000, ⓦwww.westinmalta.com. Situated on the coast at the outskirts of Paċeville in its own manicured gardens, this attractive maroon building is central but secluded, and has an impressive range of facilities, including a casino. Virtually all of the exceptionally large and fully equipped rooms have sea views. Doubles €275, breakfast included.

Windsor

Windsor Terrace, Sliema ⓣ21/346053, ⓦwww.sovereignhotels.com.mt. Situated a block away from the seafront, this overpriced outfit offers no-frills, pine-furnished rooms, including some singles, with the full range of facilities, connected by humdrum corridors. Doubles €120, breakfast included.

Guesthouse

Comfort Inn

Triq Tal-Katidral, Sliema ⓣ21/334221, ⓦwww.comfortinnmalta.com. Friendly and homely, with a cosy common living room where breakfast is served. The twelve en-suite rooms – singles, twins and triples – are compact, with cheery yellow colour schemes. Twins €40, breakfast included.

Self-catering accommodation

Dean Hamlet Complex

Triq Ross, St Julian's ⓣ21/354838, ⓦwww.deanhamlet.com.mt. This complex of studios and one-bedroom apartments serves as an ideal Paċeville base. Although the decor is uninspiring, it's all recently refurbished, and the fan-cooled apartments have full kitchens. Common facilities include a gym and pool. Studios €58; one-bedroom flats €81.50.

Hostel

Hibernia House

Triq Depiro, Sliema ⓣ21/333859, ⓦwww.nsts.org. Malta's largest hostel, offering single-sex dorms with twenty bunks, and modern, attractive and comfortable apartments, ranging from studios with two or three single beds to larger units with six single beds, rented on a shared basis or as private rooms. No breakfast included, but there's a kitchen for guests' use. Dorm beds €12, rising to €26 per bed in a twin room.

Shop

Bread Bakery

Corner of Triq San Trofimu and Triq Papa Piju V, Sliema ⓣ21/340628. Mon–Sat 5am–7pm, Sun 5am–10.30am. Traditional Maltese bakery offering a good range of crunchy, dense and inexpensive bread, from round loafs and baguettes to *ftajjar* rolls.

Cafés

Café Jubilee

18 Triq Ix-Xatt Ta' Tigne, Sliema ⓣ21/337141. Daily 8am–1am. The largest of a trio of cafés – the other two are in Valletta and Rabat, Gozo (see p.61 & p.152) – has a similar wooden interior decorated with curio prints. Snacks, coffees and quick one-plate meals give way in the evenings to a fully-fledged bar with a sophisticated range of music and a mixed clientele.

Misto

18 Triq Ix-Xatt Ta' Tigne, Sliema ⓣ21/336226. Daily 10am–10.30pm. Large, modern, minimally decorated place, with indoor and outdoor seating, which doubles up as a café and restaurant serving snacks and bigger meals, including Spanish paella (€8.75) and fried tuna served with an apple and walnut sauce and rocket salad (€15).

Offshore

4 Triq Ix-Xatt, Ta' Tigne Sliema ⓣ21/344791. Daily 7.30am–11pm.

▼ STELLA'S COFFEE SHOP

Small café with tables spilling onto the pavement, which attracts crowds of yuppies with its Maltese-style baguettes (though at inflated prices), tasteful music and good coffee.

Stella's Coffee Shop

Level 3, Plaza Shopping Complex, Triq It-Torri, Sliema ☎21/330205. Mon–Sat 9am–7pm. Despite its setting in a shopping mall, this café is friendly, unpretentious and cosy, and packed with office workers at lunchtimes, but relatively quiet otherwise. The crêpes – sweet and savoury – are excellent, as are the tortillas and Maltese-style baguettes, all of which, like the coffee, are relatively inexpensive for the location.

Restaurants

The Avenue

Triq Gort, Paceville, St Julian's ☎21/351753. Mon–Sat noon–2.30pm & 6–11.30pm, Sun 6–11.30pm. Large, cheerful place with funky decor and industrious service that manages to keep up with the groups of young Maltese who come here for the massive portions and modest prices. The large menu of mostly Sicilian dishes – from pasta and pizzas to grilled meats and fish – also includes English breakfasts, burgers and omelettes.

Barracuda

195 Triq Il-Kbira, St Julian's ☎21/331817. Daily 6.30–10.30pm. Popular with business people, with suitably formal decor and pompous service, and an extensive wine list. The cuisine is creative Italian, the tastes subtle and pastas are light on sauce. Fish dishes are adventurous and perfectly cooked. Mains around €17.

▲ BLUE ELEPHANT

Blue Elephant

Portomaso, St Julian's ☎21/383383. Daily 7–11pm. The local franchise of the Bangkok institution famous for its Royal Thai cooking serves an eclectic array of dishes, ranging from a classic spicy prawn soup to more inventive concoctions based on local ingredients, such as rabbit stir-fried in brandy and pungent Thai herbs. The service and setting are outstanding – tables are set amid lush greenery, an artificial waterfall and a pond of giant goldfish – but the small portions mean that the bill can creep up. Mains around €17.

The Kitchen

210 Triq It-Torri, Sliema ☎21/311112. Mon & Tues 7–10.30pm, Wed–Sun noon–2.30pm & 7–10.30pm. Spacious, neutrally decorated place where the pastel colours and largely empty walls put the focus on the food, which is among the best in Malta. The menu features lots of original and rich dishes such as pasta with crab, coriander, mushrooms and spring onions (€7.50) or sea bass served with a cauliflower puree, sun-dried tomatoes, olives and vanilla syrup (€12).

Il-Merill

Triq San Vinċenz, Sliema ☎21/332172. Mon–Sat 6–10pm. All rustic wooden beams, chipped walls and traditional collectibles like gas lamps, this family-run place offers inexpensive Maltese home-style cooking: hearty yet unrefined dishes such as chicken breast cooked in wine and mushrooms, or pork chops cooked with a tomato and caper sauce. All mains (around €12) are accompanied by chips and salad.

Peppino's

Triq San Ġorġ, St Julian's ☎21/373200. Mon–Sat noon–3pm & 7–10.30pm. Small and informal place serving fine continental dishes, especially French and Italian – try the rich fillet steak with pepper sauce. Tables are set on two floors: downstairs doubles as a wine bar, while upstairs is more elegant, with black tables draped with white and pink tablecloths. Around €15 for main courses.

▼ PICCOLO PADRE

Piccolo Padre

195 Triq Il-Kbira, St Julian's ☎21/344875. Daily 7–10.30pm, plus Nov–April Sun 12.30–2.45pm. Reliable and cheerful pizza and pasta house in a pleasant and informal setting. Good pasta options include spaghetti with prawns, mussels and octopus (€8.74), but it's the pizzas (all under €8) that stand out – reputedly the best in Malta – ranging from classic pizzas to ones with more adventurous toppings.

Radisson Bistro

St George's Bay, St Julian's ☎23/751198. Daily 24hr. Open to nonresidents, this good 24-hour in-hotel bistro has a limited nightly menu; among the half-a-dozen choices are salads, platters and omelettes, as well as more substantial meals such as pasta with smoked chicken, asparagus, tomatoes and cream (€6.52) and grilled fillet served with a sauce of port wine, mushrooms and tarragon and roast potatoes (€17).

Terrazza

Spinola Bay, St Julian's ☎21/384939. Mon–Sat noon–3pm & 7–11pm. *Terrazza* boasts great bay views and seating on an outdoor terrace or indoors in two funkily decorated rooms. The creative, Maltese-rooted fusion food is impeccable; the menu, which changes seasonally, may include a starter of baked Gozitan cheese coated with honey and sesame, or main dishes such as chicken breast stuffed with duck and parmesan and served with a sauce of tomatoes, cream and green mustard. Mains around €16.

▲ ŻERI'S

Wigi's Kitchen

Triq Il-Kbira, St Julian's ☎21/377504. Tues–Sat 12.30–2.45pm & 7.30–10.30pm. A small and friendly place that puts an emphasis on simple Italian cooking. The select menu, which changes daily, is based on what's fresh in the market, and could include veal with balsamic syrup and rosemary, or seared tuna served with sautéed potatoes and rocket salad. Mains around €16.

Żeri's

Portomaso, St Julian's ☎21/359599. Daily 7–11pm. Attracting a loyal clientele for its great range of avant-garde fusion dishes, the menu here is complemented by a daily-changing array of specials, which includes lots of fish, in both simple and more elaborate dishes, such as pasta with squid-ink sauce served alongside a fish fillet and mussels cooked in cream. Mains €17.

Zest

Hotel Juliani, 12 Triq San Ġorġ, St Julian's ☎21/387600. Mon–Sat 7–11.30pm. A mixed bill of Mediterranean and Asian fusion cooking, with dishes such as red snapper steamed in a banana leaf and served with Thai red curry for €17; there's also sushi and sashimi.

Bars and clubs

BJs Nightclub and Piano Bar

Triq Ball, Paċeville ☎21/377642. Daily 10pm–4am. Hosting frequent live bands – mostly soul, jazz and rock acts hailing from the 1960s to the 1980s – this place attracts an older crowd than most other Paċeville venues, with rows of sofas as well as a stand-up bar. Busiest from Thursday to Saturday, it's quiet on other nights.

Black Gold

Triq Ix-Xatt, Sliema ☎21/334808. Daily 9am–1am. The regular watering hole for yacht-hands based at Marsamxett Harbour is more of a café-style joint during the day, when it serves pub-style food. In the evenings it morphs into a more boisterous and beer-fuelled bar, especially on weekends when it's likely to stay open through until morning. The music is a mix of rock and other genres, and there are rock bands on Friday evenings.

City of London

193 Triq Il-Kbira, St Julian's ☎21/331706. Daily 10am–1am. The quiet and sunny terrace is ideal for daytime coffees and snacks, while in the evenings,

the jukebox bar attracts a mixed clientele, ranging from British expats to crowds of middle-class youngsters. On weekends they can play a rather poor, conversation-suppressing selection of loud music.

Coconut Grove

Triq Wilġa, Paċeville ☎21/333385. Daily 9pm–4am. Every day DJs play classic and commercial rock for a young crowd of Maltese teenagers who've made this their one-stop hangout. Upstairs is *Remedy* (Fri & Sat 9pm–4am), dedicated to head-banging heavy metal.

Fuego

Triq Santu Wistin, St Julian's ☎21/386746. Daily 10.30pm–4am. The most popular Latin club in Malta, with themed decor, plenty of tequilas and South American cocktails, and commercial Latin music alongside a bit of pop. One of the few places that cranks up a crowd virtually every night of the week, with a full-on party atmosphere on weekends and summer nights. There are free salsa-dancing lessons Mon–Wed 8.30–10.30pm.

Havana

Triq San Ġorġ, Paċeville ☎21/374500. Daily 9pm–4am. Despite its reputation as a pick-up joint and its jaded commercial play-list, Malta's only hip-hop club remains popular with local hip-hop followers and young tourists, particularly British and English-language students, and is usually sweaty and full on weekends.

Juuls

7 Triq San Ġużepp, St Julian's ☎21/373579. Tues–Sun 9.30pm–2am. This small bar with tasteful music – including reggae, Spanish and world music – and a friendly atmosphere attracts a crowd that's a little more mellow than the youthful headiness that dominates Paċeville. There are regular live bands (usually Wednesdays), and it tends to get rather busy

▼ FUEGO

on weekends, when it's usually open very late.

Muddy Waters

56 Triq Il-Kbira, St Julian's ☎21/374155. Daily 5pm–1am. A rock and blues bar, busiest when they have an occasional live band, but otherwise a local hangout that's pleasantly full at weekends and quiet on week nights.

Places

Triq Ball, Paċeville ☎21/318055. June–Sept daily 10pm–4am; Oct–May Wed & Fri–Sat 10pm–4am. This spacious bar is chilled on week nights, but livelier at weekends, with DJs playing house (sometimes hard-house or techno) for a young crowd of clubbers who use it as a warm-up venue if there's a big rave on elsewhere. It's a good place to scope out the latest trends in the local clubbing scene.

Ryan's Irish Pub

Triq Wied Ghomor, St Julian's ☎21/350680. Mon–Thurs 4pm–2am, Fri–Sun 10am–4am. Standard, attractive Irish pub that is popular with a young crowd of locals and tourists. The music is mostly house and R&B, and also occasionally some popular Irish tunes during the week, but the large TV screen dominates the attention when important European football games are on. There are sporadic performances from a diverse selection of live bands on Friday nights.

The Scotsman Pub

Triq San Ġorġ, St Julian's ☎21/353660. Daily 11am–2am. The closest thing in Malta to an

▲ PAĊEVILLE AT NIGHT

English pub, offering fish and chips and roast Sunday dinners and attracting a generally British clientele. Exhibit your singing prowess at the funny and inebriated karaoke nights (Tues, Thurs, Sat & Sun), or indulge in nostalgia at the popular Elvis-themed Friday nights.

Simon's Pub

115–116 Triq Depiro, Sliema ☎21/317008. Tues–Sun 11am–1pm & 8.30pm–1am. Friendly little den bristling with delightful bric-a-brac and football memorabilia, with additional outdoor seating on an attractive terrace. The inexpensive drinks, served in generous measures, attract a regular core clientele, and its 26 cocktails are among the best you'll find in Malta. Music is mostly rock, with due exposure given to local bands.

Mdina, Rabat and the south central coast

With everything from Malta's oldest and best-preserved town to comparatively lush valleys and the rugged heights of the coast, as well as Malta's best sandy beaches, this region has a distinct feel and allure. It should be a major draw on any itinerary, starting with Mdina, the aristocratic old capital ringed by early medieval fortifications. Rabat, the adjoining town and once a Mdina suburb, has an eclectic mix of underground historical sights from the same period, and to the west Malta's largest woodland is the most verdant of several valleys bisecting the island's highest plateau. The highlands continue to Il-Kunċizzjoni before tumbling down to Fomm Ir-Rih, a wildly beautiful bay. Further north, beyond Mġarr, Malta's top trio of sandy beaches are cut in dramatic gulfs of clay slopes crowned by cliffs.

Mdina

Built on a ridge and ringed by fortifications, aristocratic Mdina is one of Malta's major highlights. Established by the Phoenicians, this tiny, winningly attractive walled town was Malta's first urban settlement, and served as the island's capital until Valletta took over in 1571. It's easy to detect Mdina's medieval history beneath its Baroque makeover (courtesy of the Knights in 1722), and its maze of narrow, twisting alleys have kept modernity at bay. Virtually car-free and with just four hundred inhabitants, it falls deathly quiet by night – when it's at its most evocative for a walk, your footsteps echoing down the alleys – while during the day it's a regular haunt for the tour groups. Nonetheless, a wander through Mdina to soak up the atmosphere is unmissable at any time.

▲ MDINA ALLEYWAY

The Main Gate and Pjazza San Publiju

Mdina. The primary Baroque gate through Mdina's fortifications was built by the Knights in 1724 as part of a restoration

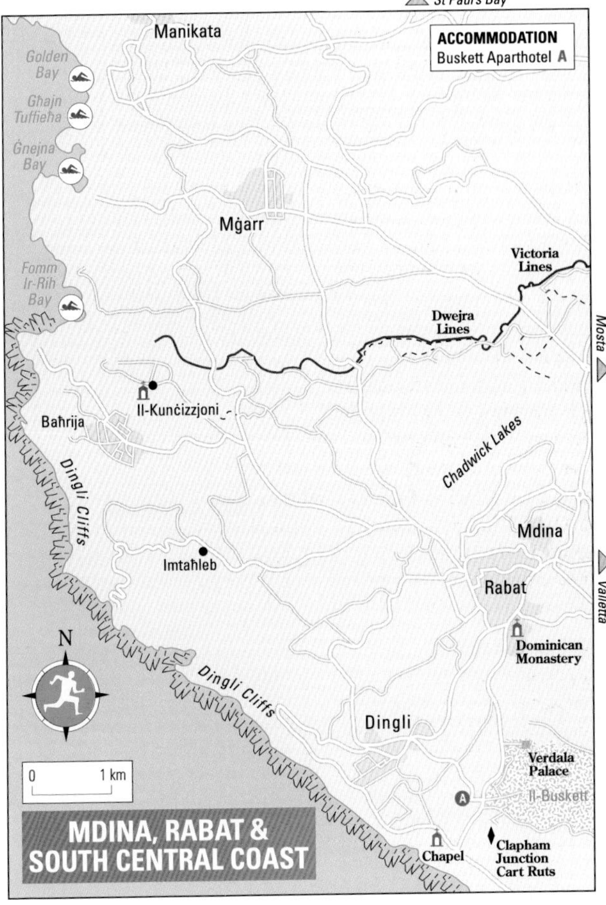

programme overseen by Grand Master Manoel de Vilhena, whose coat of arms (a lion and a sword, symbolizing his eminence as an outstanding naval warrior) sit at the top of the gate; the internal facade is crowned by statues of Mdina's patron saints Paul, Publius and Agatha. As part of the restoration, de Vilhena shifted the gate east (you can still see the outline of its predecessor to one side) so that it would lead directly to the planned Magisterial Palace and open onto Pjazza San Publiju.

Magisterial Palace

Pjazza San Publiju, Mdina. The fourth and last of the Grand Masters' palaces built in Malta, in 1724, the Magisterial Palace was designed by the French architect Charles François de Medion. The palace is set on two floors around a central courtyard; Grand Master de Vilhena spent the summers here, away from public life in Valletta,

Visiting Mdina and Rabat

Mdina and Rabat are reached on buses #80 from Valletta, #65 from Sliema, and #86 from Buġibba. Bus #81 from Valletta passes Mdina and Rabat and continues to Il-Buskett and Dingli Cliffs. There are two car parks between Mdina and Rabat.

and his bust and coat of arms are mounted above the main door of another courtyard to the front of the building. The palace's interior was first pared down when it was converted into a hospital under British rule, and its splendour was further ruined in 1973 when it was reopened as the **Museum of Natural History** (daily 9am–5pm; €2.33; ⓣ21/455951, ⓦwww.heritagemalta.org), a worn-out display of bits and pieces that is hardly worth the effort. You can get a look at the palace's facade, which survives intact, from the first courtyard.

Mdina Dungeons

Pjazza San Publiju, Mdina ⓣ21/450267. Daily 9.30am–4.30pm. €4. The former prisons underneath the Magisterial Palace serve as a suitable home for this gruesome if mildly diverting museum, which aims to re-create various acts of torture that occurred in Malta over the ages. The graphic life-sized tableaux depicting different torture methods under Malta's various rulers (St Agatha's breasts being hacked off by the Romans and the like), are given extra gravity by the fact that many of the acts took place in the rooms now occupied by the reconstructions.

St Paul's Cathedral

Pjazza San Pawl, Mdina Mon–Fri 9.30am–4.30pm, Sat 9.30am–3.30pm; €2.50 for the Cathedral and museum. Sun open for mass in the morning and late afternoon; free. The principal focus of a visit to Mdina, St Paul's Cathedral is the finest ecclesiastical building in Malta – a majestic, beautifully proportioned architectural set-piece that dominates the skyline for miles around. Dedicated to Malta's most venerated saint, it was built to replace an earlier

▼ MAGISTERIAL PALACE

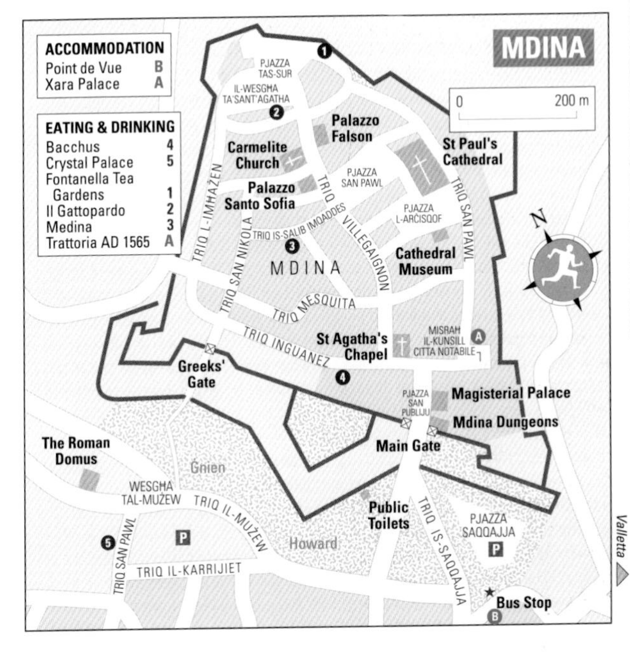

cathedral which collapsed in the earthquake of 1693. The ecclesiastical authorities saw this as an ideal opportunity to build something far grander, demolishing the surrounding houses to create an open square, and commissioning the best-known Maltese architect of the time, Lorenzo Gafa, to design it. It's acknowledged as Gafa's masterpiece, although he never saw it finished, dying before it was inaugurated in 1702. Unlike his peers, Gafa shunned the ornateness of Baroque in favour of composition and setting, and here he created a grand presence by designing a facade with square proportions, the width equal to the height, a stylistic technique that is unusual in churches. This is topped by an elegant octagonal dome, decorated with handsome stone scrolls and framed by squat bell towers; both dome and bell towers seem, in their sudden blast of voluptuousness, like separate appendages, another stylistic technique associated with Gafa's works.

The **interior** also employs skilful spatial amplification, appearing higher and more cavernous than is suggested from the outside. However, in contrast to St John's Co-Cathedral's celebration of knightly vanity, Mdina's cathedral pays homage to clerical ascetic steadfastness, with just five bronze busts, attached to the piers dividing the nave, commemorating notable Maltese bishops. The 134 variegated marble tombstones that patchwork the floor of the nave mark the graves of other venerated clerics, while overhead, the three ceiling frescoes depicting a preaching

A Mdina walking tour

The individual sights detailed in this guide should form the focus of a walk around Mdina to take in its handsome palaces – once the homes of Malta's nobility – and the town's well-preserved medieval ambience. Just past the main gate, **Triq Villegaignon** is the main road, cutting across the town and featuring the largest palaces. It opens into Pjazza San Pawl, and just beyond the square, Mdina's oldest building, **Palazzo Santo Sofia**, is recognizable from the street-tunnel that cuts through its ground floor. The ground floor of the two-storey house itself dates from 1233, while its upper floor is a fine example of Siculo-Norman architecture, a hybrid of Norman and Sicilian styles found only in Malta. The highlight of the Siculo-Norman style are the ornate mullioned windows – double-arched windows divided by a column and framed by pronounced pitched arches which are in turn fringed by carvings of either leafy motifs or a raised design of zigzag masonry. Triq Villegaignon eventually ends at Pjazza Tas-Sur, a pleasant clearing set behind the ramparts of the fortifications. The square is backed by elegant houses and fronted by ficus trees which offer pools of shade from where to take in the view from one of Malta's highest points: just beyond the walls terraced fields step down to the central agricultural plains, and on to the urban conurbation of the northwest coast, a sweep stretching from the Three Cities to Buġibba.

West of Pjazza Tas-Sur, **Triq L-Imħażen** cuts south, and between it and the parallel Triq Villegaignon there is a maze of meandering alleyways that hold more ancient buildings, some of which sport the characteristic mullioned windows of the Siculo-Norman style. Many of these buildings also have absorbing coats of arms and elaborate bronze door-knockers that are moulded into various motifs. At its end, Triq L-Imħażen leads to Triq San Nikola, which itself leads out of the walls via the town's second gate, the simple **Greeks' Gate** – named after the Greek community that lived in this part of town in the Middle Ages.

St Paul are appropriately simple and solemn. The nave's six side chapels are also modest affairs, as are the paintings on the inside of the dome. More dramatic are the two large and atmospheric paintings by Mattia Preti in the chancel: the *Conversion of St Paul* serves as the altarpiece, while the *Shipwreck of St Paul* decorates the apse above. The two chapels flanking the altar hold more rich embellishments, mostly the work of Maltese artist Francesco Zahra (1710–73). The various lunettes and cupola paintings are Zahra's masterworks, a powerful set grouped under the themes of the Triumph of the Eucharist and Triumph of the Cross.

▼ SICULO-NORMAN WINDOWS, PALAZZO SANTO SOFIA

Cathedral Museum

Pjazza Ta' L-Arċisqof, Mdina ☎21/454697. Same ticket and hours as Cathedral. Across the road, the Cathedral Museum is a repository for the cathedral's moveable arts accumulated over the centuries. Housed in the former Diocesan Seminary, a two-storey Baroque pile built in 1733–40, the Cathedral

Museum's artworks and historical relics constitute a valuable and memorable collection, and the largest private museum in Malta. The richest pickings are on the upper floor, where Catholic art dominates; in the first hall, Fra Salvatore di Bisignano's embossed Choral Books from 1576, which open to the size of a coffee table, are especially worth seeking out. In the adjoining oval chapel, built in situ during the Seminary's construction, the Annunciation altarpiece by French artist Antoine de Favray is technically good but emotionally mute; more absorbing are the twelfth-century Romanesque chalice and intricately enamelled Byzantine altar stone displayed in a recessed cabinet. Another highlight is the fantastic and intricate series of 53 woodcuts and copperplates by Albrecht Dürer, yet the most outstanding exhibit is in the adjacent hall, where a chessboard marble floor creates a soothing tableaux of perspective for the *Polyptych of St Paul* by Luis Borrassa, a large and well-crafted fifteenth-century piece that's stirring in its sombrely medieval mood and symbolism.

Palazzo Falson

Triq Villegaignon, Mdina ⓣ21/454512, ⓦwww.palazzofalson.com. Tues–Sun 10am–5pm. €10.

Originally built in the thirteenth century in Siculo-Norman style, Palazzo Falson was tinkered with throughout the centuries, and the first floor and its mullioned windows were added in the sixteenth century. Now it's a fascinating museum that serves as a double attraction: the ground floor, dating from

▲ STATUE OF THE MADONNA OUTSIDE THE CARMELITE CHURCH ON TRIQ VILLEGAIGNON

the original construction, showcases some of the interior features of Siculo-Norman architecture while the exhibits spread thickly throughout the building constitute a priceless array of historical art. The art was amassed by Olof Gollcher, who bought the house in 1927 and spent his vast wealth, inherited from a family who owned a shipping line, on filling his house with art and historical objects, many of them scavenged during his travels. Now Gollcher's bounty fills every space of the first floor, where the living quarters have been re-created, shedding light on a character who was both exuberant and bohemian – the dining room, for example, is decked out with silver tableware, yet the bedroom next door is relatively restrained with its quaint poster bed and trim cupboards.

▲ PALAZZO FALSON

Moving through the first floor you'll pass cases full of models of galleys, including some made from silver, as well as jewellery (including lots of Maltese crosses) and an array of watches (note the ten-hour dial watch that was made during the French Revolution and may be one of the few that still exist). More notable are the paintings in the living room; highlights include Mattia Preti's *Lucretia Stabbing Herself*, Edward Lear's take on the idyllic and tranquil coastal landscapes in Malta, and the excellent four-piece study of different seasons by Nicolas Poussin (each feature a haunted-looking small boy doing something symbolizing the season). An audioguide included with the entry ticket helps explain the displays.

The ground floor, meanwhile, survives in its original simplicity, set on bare-stone walls and stone tiles with interior arches creating a medieval atmosphere that is most vivid in the kitchen with its brass pots, large metal oven and beautifully tiled fireplace.

The Roman Domus

Il-Wesgħa Tal-Mużew, Mdina ⓣ21/454125, ⓦwww.heritagemalta.org. Daily 9am–5pm. €4.66. A repository for most of Malta's diminutive collection of Roman relics, the Roman Domus museum is built around the remains of its star attraction, a Roman villa that was unearthed in 1881. It was built in around 50 AD, and is one of 25 Roman villas in Malta that are thought to have served as the homesteads of large agricultural estates, probably producing olive oil. The location of this building, on the outskirts of Mdina (then Malta's de facto capital), as well as the statues discovered within of Emperor Claudius and his mother Antonia, suggest that it belonged to a senior Roman figure. Now only the peristyle, with a splendid mosaic floor, survives from the original house. There are also other fragments of mosaic in the museum, the most striking of which is a rather disturbing depiction of an open-mouthed woman seemingly gripped with fear. But the rest of the museum's collection is pedestrian: Roman amphorae, an olive press and fragments of columns and bits of statuary, all interpreted by informative panels.

Rabat

Five minutes' walk south of Mdina along Triq San Pawl brings you to Rabat's town square, to which Mdina's walls had stretched until Arab rule (870–1090 AD). The Arabs rebuilt the fortifications on a smaller scale for better defensibility, in effect creating a new suburb ("rabat" means suburb in Arabic) which eventually grew into a town. Rabat's main sights – the catacombs – date back to the time when Rabat was part of Mdina, when early Christians buried their dead outside the city walls. Rabat is now also a distinct, proud town whose inhabitants speak a separate dialect, and many of whom remain farmers working the fields in the fertile valleys outside town. These countless valleys, reached via narrow country roads, offer rural serenity and quaint scenery in the form of old hamlets and farmhouses, and, if you have a car, they are good places to explore on a sunny day.

St Paul's Church and grotto

Misraħ Il-Paroċċa, Rabat. Mon–Sat 9am–5pm. Free. Rabat's town square is dominated by St Paul's Church, which stands on a site where a church is known to have existed since 1372, though the present Baroque building dates from 1653. Designed by Francesco Bounamici, who introduced Baroque architecture to Malta, it has an unusually wide, squat facade that tapers to an elegant peak in wavy curvaceous scrolls, while the simple dome, rebuilt in the nineteenth century, and bell towers are set well back from the street. For a church with such a lengthy history, the interior is surprisingly bare and bland – the only

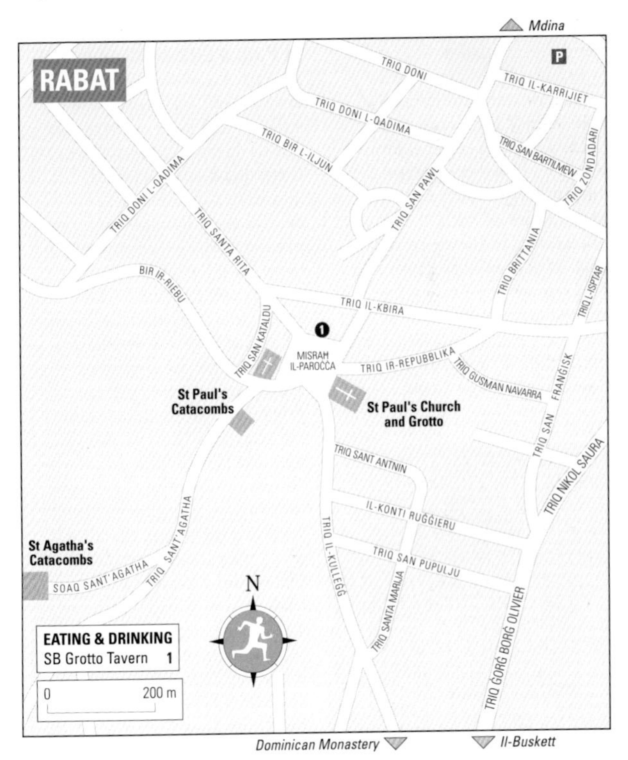

▲ ST PAUL'S GROTTO

noteworthy features are the three seventeenth-century altarpieces: from bottom to top, a somewhat clichéd depiction of St Paul's shipwreck by Stefano Erardi, a calculated, reserved St Publius by Mattia Preti, and an abstract Eucharist by Francesco Zahra. Below the church is the cave where St Paul is said to have been interned during his three-month stint in Malta in 60 AD while awaiting his transfer to Rome to stand trial. It's a small, dampish and disappointingly dull grotto, yet the association with St Paul made it a pilgrimage site during the Knights' time. Now more popular with tour groups than with pilgrims, there are a few pieces of decoration to admire, including Melchiorre Gafa's 1667 statue of St Paul.

▼ ST PAUL'S CATACOMBS

St Paul's Catacombs

Triq Sant' Agatha, Rabat ⓣ21/454562, ⓦwww.heritagemalta.org. Daily 9am–5pm. €4.66. A claustrophobic and dark maze of early Christian burial chambers dug in the fourth and fifth centuries, St Paul's Catacombs offer an absorbing insight into early burial methods. Set on a number of different terraced levels, the 1000-odd sarcophagi occupy every conceivable space. Just through the entrance, the complex starts with a primitive chapel of a stone-cut altar and two circular tables with benches, where the congregation gathered to pray, mourn and feast during ritual burials. From here, there's no straightforward way to tour the labyrinthine passageways – all of them end in a blank rock wall – so the best approach is simply to wander around, constantly doubling back on yourself. Now that the lids of the sarcophagi have been removed, it's possible to distinguish the different types of tomb – loculi are small rectangular recesses cut into the walls, generally used for infants and children; arcosolium tombs are dug directly into the ground; while canopied table tombs consist of a series of graves alongside each other about a metre above the floor, on shelves framed by arches.

St Agatha's Catacombs

Sqaq Sant' Agatha, Rabat ☎21/454419. Mon–Fri 9am–4.30pm, Sat 9am–12.30pm. €2.50. St Agatha's was in use from the Byzantine era (400 AD) through to the seventeenth century. It's a large complex, with two hundred graves for adults and three hundred for children, as well as a crypt where St Agatha hid in 249 AD after she fled Roman persecution in Catania. A tour of the section that is open to the public starts at the crypt's two adjoining chapels. The smaller one is dedicated to the Madonna, while the larger chapel, with a freestanding altar, has several colourful ancient frescoes: the earliest three, nearest the door, are Byzantine representations of the Madonna, St Agatha and St Paul, while the others, Gothic in style and dating from the fourteenth and fifteenth centuries, depict St Agatha in various poses. From the crypt, the catacombs stretch deep into the rock in progressive sections, starting from the earliest section, a pagan burial chamber complete with the almost intact original skeletons in open sarcophagi, and leading to a sixth-century Christian burial section hollowed around a small, oval chapel with a primitive altar and a fresco altarpiece rich in symbolism – the shell represents heaven, the pigeons the soul and the tree, life.

Dominican Monastery

Triq Ġorġ Borg Olivier, Rabat. Daily dawn–dusk. Free. Malta's order of Dominican monks arrived here from Sicily in 1450, and built their convent over a cave dedicated to Our Lady of the Grotto, which had become a place of pilgrimage in the Middle Ages after a hunter claimed he had an apparition of the Madonna inside it. The original convent building was renovated and expanded and a larger church added in 1683. The public are allowed access to the courtyard and cloister, and the convent church (the monks – now numbering only twenty – occupy living quarters on the upper floor). The elegant cloister features a ribbed barrel-vaulted ceiling, while balustrades and loggias overlook the courtyard garden, with its groves of orange trees criss-crossed by pathways. Entrance to the church is through a doorway in the cloister. Dedicated to Our Lady of the Grotto, its interior is simple and bathed

▼ DOMINICAN MONASTERY

▲ IL-BUSKETT GARDENS AND VERDALA PALACE

in light; near the front door a staircase leads down to the original grotto, now a separate chapel where elder townsfolk gather in the afternoons to say the Rosary.

Il-Buskett and Verdala Palace

Triq Il-Buskett, Il Buskett. Bus #81 from Valletta and Rabat. Il-Buskett – Malta's only mature, self-generating woodland – makes a great spot for a picnic and a stroll. Created by the Knights in the seventeenth century, it served as the private hunting grounds around Verdala Palace, which was commissioned in 1586 by Grand Master Hugues Loubenx de Verdalle as a country retreat. These days, the palace is the Maltese president's summer residence, and closed to visitors, but you can get a glimpse of its turreted exterior rising above the grove of Aleppo pines that surround it. The Il-Buskett woodlands are open to visitors, though, and are reached via a snaking road immediately west of the palace. This ends at a car park, from where paths branch in different directions, including one that winds down the valley into the dense web of Aleppo pines, Mediterranean oaks, olives and carobs. Overhung by gnarled, hollowed tree-trunks, the path follows the meanderings of a small stream in the wet winter season, and you might see the passerine songbirds which come here to drink. In September, flocks of migrating birds of prey roost in the trees and make good birdwatching (see p.170).

Fomm Ir-Rih Bay

No public transport. One of Malta's wildest and most beautiful spots, hemmed in by cliffs and

Clapham Junction cart ruts

Named by British archeologists after the similarly intricate web of railway lines at Clapham Junction station in London, this jumble of parallel grooves cut into the rocky plateau west of Il-Buskett comprises the densest network of such ruts in Malta (similar channels are found all over the Mediterranean, but are most numerous here). The cart ruts pose an archeological puzzle, since no satisfactory explanation exists as to their origin. The most accepted – although hazy – hypothesis is that they were made by wheeled carts during the Bronze Age (2000–1400 BC), but the problem with this theory is that the ruts have no apparent destination or pattern: some of them peter out, while others disappear into the sea or halt at cliff-edges – even the tiny islet of Filfla (see p.128) off Malta's south coast is webbed by cart ruts. The mystery is deepened by the fact that in some places, such as Clapham Junction, multiple sets of ruts cross over one another. The debate on the possible date and origin of the cart ruts continues, with explanations ranging from the simple (that they were water channels, for example) to the bizarre (that they were made by aliens).

Il-Kunċizzjoni coastal walk

The rugged and wild coastal landscape west of Rabat offers some wonderfully scenic walking, though you'll need your own transport to get here. This isolated stretch of coast, the highest area in Malta, offers spectacular views over to the undulating ridges of northwestern Malta, and all the way to Gozo, with the dramatic Ta Ċenċ cliffs on the horizon. A short and easy walk begins at Il-Kunċizzjoni (signposted from Rabat), a tiny farming hamlet established in 1731. The main approach road into the village passes a small chapel, then peters out after 500m at a small clearing where you can park. From here, a path leads inland for 200m, at a slight incline to a rocky bluff that marks the tail end of the Great Fault. This geological fault divides Malta along its centre, and the British built the Victoria Lines defensive wall along it in the 1870s. The wall peters out here at the bluff, which is backed by crumbling defensive underground positions. An opening in the wall leads down the hill past fields for about 1km, where it reaches the cliff that girdles the large dramatic bay below, Fomm Ir-Rih. You can double back here, or follow the steep path down the slope to the bay.

clay slopes eroded into dramatic gullies, the pebbly beach at Fomm Ir-Rih is a good spot for snorkelling on calm days (take care to avoid the potentially ankle-twisting rocks in the shallows, though). When the wind is blowing from the north or northwest, however, the bay seems true to its name, which means "the mouth of the wind" – the usually clear, azure water becomes metallic and opaque, and crashing waves make swimming unthinkable. To get to Fomm Ir-Rih from Il-Kunċizzjoni or Rabat, follow the signposts to the small modern town of Baħrija. Drive straight through along the town's main road, and take the first right; some 2km further, after the road starts meandering downhill, take another right which ends in a small car park. From here a footpath, which runs precariously along a ledge at the start, descends to the pebbly shore – it's around ten minutes' walk from the car park.

Ġnejna Bay

No public transport. Beyond Mġarr, a small, uninteresting town founded in the nineteenth century, the road continues to Ġnejna Bay, a large scenic bay

▼ ĠNEJNA BAY

▲ GOLDEN BAY

nestled in a trough at the mouth of a valley. The small swathe of orange-coloured sand backed by clear and calm water is popular with families in summer. The bay itself is enclosed by dramatic clay slopes crowned by craggy amber cliffs and, on the highest vantage point, one of the Knights' seventeenth-century coastal defence towers. Canoes and other watersports equipment are available to rent, and a kiosk sells refreshments and snacks all year round. The road to Ġnejna Bay from Mġarr is well signposted, and there's a car park backing on to the sand.

Għajn Tuffieħa and Golden Bay

Bus #347 from Valletta and #652 from Sliema and Buġibba. North of Ġnejna Bay, and accessed by a separate road from Mġarr or from St Paul's Bay (see p.107), are Malta's most scenic sandy beaches. Divided by a gently rounded peninsula, the gorgeous stretches of sand, easy access, and stunning natural beauty make these twin beaches two of Malta's most popular. Both have outlets offering watersports, sun loungers and umbrellas, as well as snack bars.

The southerly of the two, **Għajn Tuffieħa**, is the more dramatic, with the typical clay slopes and cliffs of the coastal landscape hereabouts. A flight of stairs from the car park on top of the cliff leads to the narrow crescent-shaped sandy shore, lapped by water that takes on the warm auburn colour of the seabed. It's a popular haunt for image-conscious twenty-something Maltese, making it a whirl of designer swimsuits and flashy sunglasses.

Golden Bay is partly spoiled by a multi-storey hotel that dominates the bay from its cliff-top perch and, nearer the sand, the road and car park that reach down to the beach. This easier access means it gets more crowded than Għajn Tuffieħa in summer, attracting a mix of young Maltese and tourists.

Hotels

Buskett Aparthotel

Il-Buskett, Rabat ⓣ21/454266, ⓕ21/455949. A good budget base in a rural location near Il-Buskett, though you'll need your own transport to get here. The three basic double rooms have fans and shared bathrooms, while the thirteen spacious but stark one- to three- bedroom apartments have full kitchens. Doubles €28, one-bedroom apartments €35.

Xara Palace

Misraħ Il-Kunsill Ċitta Notabile, Mdina ⓣ21/450560, ⓦwww.xarapalace.com.mt. Set in a beautifully restored eighteenth-century palace, this atmospheric, intimate and impossibly romantic hotel is possibly Malta's best. It's decorated throughout with antique furniture and portraits, while rooms have the full range of modern facilities and Jacuzzis; those at the back have excellent views of northern Malta. Doubles from €235.

Guesthouse

Point de Vue

5 Pjazza Saqqaja, Rabat ☎21/454117. A townhouse outside the walls of Mdina, where the twelve large rooms – clean, spartan and bright, with attached toilets and showers – come in singles, twins, doubles and triples. Air-conditioning units are planned for the rooms, which will lead to a rise in prices. Doubles €56, breakfast included.

Cafés

Crystal Palace

90 Triq San Pawl, Rabat ☎21/453323. Daily 4am–8pm. An old-style *pastizzi* joint, cluttered with Formica tables, offering some of Malta's best *pastizzi* – puff-pastry pockets stuffed with mashed peas or ricotta – as well as hot drinks and alcohol. Cheap and filling, and made with a lard-heavy dough, a couple of *pastizzi* are more than enough.

Fontanella Tea Gardens

1 Pjazza Tas-Sur, Mdina ☎21/450208. Daily 10am–7pm for café; 7pm–midnight for wine bar. With tables spread out over the parapet of the Mdina fortifications and with dreamy views over Malta, this is a great place for a daytime coffee and cake. With the fortifications majestically lit and lights twinkling into the distance, it's even better at night when it morphs into a wine bar serving wine, other drinks and platters of finger-food.

Il Gattopardo

20 Triq Villegaigon, Mdina ☎21/451213. Mon–Sat 11.30am–3pm & 8–10.30pm. A memorable café in a great setting in the beautiful courtyards and rooms of an old townhouse, decorated with tasteful art pieces and home to rotating art exhibitions. The mostly Greek menu centres on light, delicious and inexpensive one-plate meals such as vine leaves stuffed with rice and pine nuts, and other classics.

Restaurants

Bacchus

Triq Inguanez, Mdina ☎21/454981. Daily noon–3pm & 6–11pm. Set in an atmospheric fifteenth-century ammunition store

▼ MEDINA

▲ SB GROTTO TAVERN

built by the Knights, with tables in the leafy garden during summer, the location is naturally romantic, and the menu, which changes seasonally, is full of hearty French dishes (around €15) such as pork tenderloin with artichokes, curried mussel and vegetable soup, or baked seabass with a salt crust.

Medina

Triq Is-Salib Imqaddes, Mdina ☎21/454004. Mon–Sat 7–10.30pm.
Sublimely set in a restored townhouse, with tables spilling into a courtyard canopied by climbing vines. The menu, which changes regularly, is full of interesting French dishes such as Wonton duck served on a bed of spicy lentils and a sauce made of cream, peaches and raisins. About €16 for main courses.

SB Grotto Tavern

Misraħ Il-Paroċċa, Rabat ☎21/455138. June–Sept Mon–Sat noon–2.30pm & Tues–Sat 7–10.30pm; Oct–May Tues–Sun noon–2.30pm & 7–10pm.
A large restaurant set in a cellar, with three themed rooms, offering creative French dishes (around €15) ranging from chicken breast stuffed with prawn mousse to snails baked in butter and garlic, and the best Swiss fondue in Malta, for €15.50 per person. The complex also has a cave decked out as a wine bar, serving wine and antipasti in a comfortable setting.

Trattoria AD 1565

Misraħ Il-Kunsill Ċitta Notabile, Mdina ☎21/450560. Daily 11am–10.30pm.
A bustling place located in a barrel-vaulted chamber and outdoors in the atmospheric square, the trattoria of the *Xara Palace* hotel serves a large range of inexpensive Italian and French dishes and snacks, including good pizzas and a range of pasta dishes and main courses, all competently cooked.

Central Malta

A genteel trio of towns – collectively known as the Three Villages – Attard, Balzan and Lija are laidback, leafy places which are as desirable addresses today as they were when the Knights built country retreats here, all with extensive gardens. Ġnien Sant Anton – a Grand Master's former garden – is now Malta's largest and plushest public garden. Other sights scattered around the towns, which can be seen in a half-day's stroll, include the elegant medieval parish churches, fine old townhouses towering over the narrow alleyways and many delightful Baroque architectural features that make the Three Villages a watercolourist's playground. Palazzo Parisio, the swankiest palace open to the public, is situated northwest at the town of Naxxar, and Mosta, the adjacent town, holds the bulbous Mosta Dome, claimed to be Europe's third-largest.

Attard

Fringed by grand detached villas, the Three Villages are characterized by a core of shaded alleys clustered quaintly around medieval parish churches. The focal point of a visit to Attard is **St Mary's Church** (daily 7–10am & 5–7pm; free), set in the compact, quiet pedestrianized Pjazza Tommaso Dingli. Designed in 1613 in the form of a Latin cross, the small Renaissance-style building is the most architecturally outstanding pre-Baroque church in Malta, with a simplicity that belies its beauty. It has a single turret-like bell tower and three domes, the main cupola flanked by two smaller ones, their summits painted a striking pomegranate red. Inside, square panels covering the domes and vault add textural detail, while Renaissance flower motifs frame the few paintings on the walls of the nave; more striking are the enchanting statues of saints mounted high in recessed niches in the chancel.

Five minutes' walk north, along Triq Il-Kbira and then Triq Sant' Anton, takes you to Attard's other notable sight, **Ġnien Sant' Anton** (daily: June–Sept 7am–6pm; Oct–May

Visiting the Three Villages

The best way to explore the Three Villages is on foot, and with only a kilometre or so between each centre, it's hard to determine where one community ends and the next begins. All three are served by bus #40 from Valletta. From Buġibba, the #427 passes through Mosta en route to the Three Villages, and a raft of Valletta-originating buses (all buses heading to the northwestern destinations of St Paul's, Mellieħa, and Ċirkewwa) pass through Mosta's town centre. Naxxar is only connected to Valetta via buses #55 and #56.

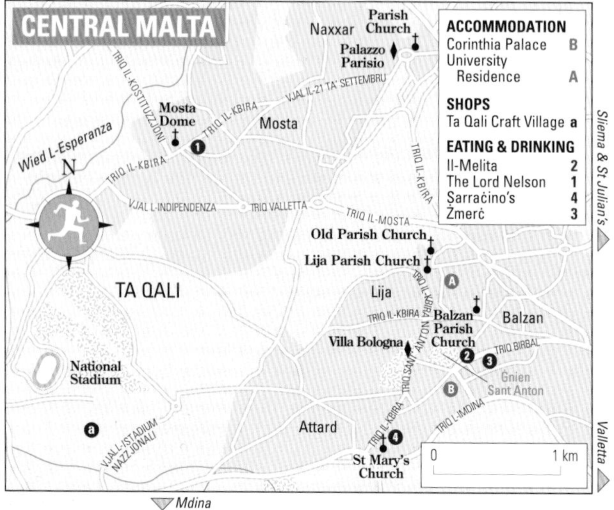

7am–5pm; free). Sant Anton Palace and its garden were built by the French Grand Master Antoine de Paule in 1623 as his private retreat. It subsequently housed other Grand Masters, as well as various governors under British rule; it's now the official residence of Malta's president, so not open to the public. However, the large garden, enclosed by high perimeter walls and still retaining the intimate feel of a private estate, is open to visitors, and makes a lovely spot for a stroll. Dotted with towering palms, oaks, ficus, cypresses and citrus groves, the garden is laid out around a grid pattern of cobbled paths, with every transverse intersection decorated by a stone fountain and a pond that's home to turtles, ducks, swans and goldfish.

▼ ĠNIEN SANT' ANTON, ATTARD

Lija and Balzan

Northeast of Attard, the narrow and straight Triq Sant' Anton features a string of large, affluent-looking houses. Dating from the eighteenth century, the older ones boast intricate Baroque facades, while those dating from Malta's period of British rule have rather English front gardens and bay windows. Some sport turret-like lookout towers that illustrate the siege mentality of their original owners, who clearly felt vulnerable living outside Malta's fortified towns. There's little focus for your exploration in nondescript Balzan; it's best to press on along Triq Il-Kbira to the centre of Lija. Here, Triq Sant' Andrija is another atmospheric alley of seventeenth-century Baroque townhouses, and the network of alleyways northwest of Triq Sant' Andrija and west of the main church represent the Three Villages at their most evocative. Picturesque alleys branch off the winding streets, with the occasional clump of bougainvillea lending a splash of colour to the facades of the handsome old houses.

Lija's central square, Misraħ It-Trasfigurazzjoni, is dominated by the parish church. Dating from the 1690s, although comparatively restrained in size it's a remarkable set piece raised on a podium with two obelisks framing its facade. The square is a major draw during the town feast, held each August (see p.166), when one of the best pyrotechnic shows in the world is staged here. North of the square, in Triq Sir Ugo Mifsud Bonniċi, there's some more absorbing architecture in the form of Lija's Old Parish Church of St Saviour, a modest early-sixteenth-century rectangular building, with an interesting dome that – as one of Malta's earliest – forms a stylistic bridge between the pitched roofs of vernacular medieval chapels and the grander churches of the Baroque period.

Mosta Dome

Pjazza Rotunda, Mosta. Daily 5am–noon & 3–8pm. Free. Buses

▲ LIJA STREET

#56 and #58 from Valletta, #65 from Sliema, or #86 and #427 from Buġibba. Despite its characterless urban sprawl, the town of Mosta is squarely on the tourist trail for its nineteenth-century parish church of Santa Marija, better known as the Mosta Dome. Visible from vantage points all around Malta, the huge rotunda – claimed to be Europe's third-largest – is undoubtedly impressive, but the feverish hype surrounding it says more about the Maltese awe of anything gigantic than about its true artistic importance. The architect Georges Grognet de Vasse designed the church with a circular (instead of a more usual cruciform) floor-plan, and also incorporated elements of the Pantheon, particularly noticeable in the portico with its twin rows of six columns on which the bell

▲ MOSTA DOME

towers seem like awkward appendages. The design was derided by the archbishop of the time, but building began regardless in 1833 and took 27 years. Illuminated by sixteen windows and a lantern light, the cavernous interior features a marble floor with an inlaid geometric pattern, while its coffered ceiling is decorated with gilded stone-carved flowers on a blue background which swirl around the yawning dome. Giuseppe Cali painted the murals above the side-altars at the beginning of the twentieth century, but they are too high up to display his abilities to any effect. Left of the altar, the sacristy is dedicated to recounting, in pictures and rambling text, what has been dubbed the "Miracle of St Mary". During World War II, as a three-hundred-strong congregation waited for mass, a Luftwaffe bomb pierced the dome and skittered along the floor; when it failed to explode, the parishioners put the episode down to divine intervention.

Palazzo Parisio

Pjazza Vittorja, Naxxar ⓣ21/412461, ⓦwww.palazzoparisio.com. Mon–Fri 9am–4pm. €8.15. Bus #55 from Valletta, or #65 from Sliema. The sole draw of the town of Naxxar, this nineteenth-century palace in the main square is Malta's most opulent aristocratic home, a fantastic and overwhelming construction of frothy plasterwork that stands testament to the vanity of the Maltese aristocracy during British colonial rule. Built in the early nineteenth century by Sicilian aristocrats, the palace underwent a seven-year upgrade after it was acquired by Marquis Giuseppe Scicluna in 1898, and the extravagant interior modifications seem designed solely to impress, with rooms dedicated to billiards and the Marquis' carriage, as well as a private chapel and a "ladies' musical room". The informative guided tours, led on the hour (though suspended in the afternoon on quiet days), provide plenty of detail on the art works and the owner's princely lifestyle. Many of the decorative features were custom-made in Italy – the coping over the banisters is made from a slab of marble so huge that it took three attempts to transport it here (the ship sank in the first attempt, and the stone was damaged in the second), and needed forty donkeys to haul it up from the port. The

Italian artist Filippo Venuti was commissioned to execute the paintings that decorate each room, as well as the sumptuous ceiling fresco on the first-floor landing that depicts the history of Malta, offering a romanticized take on the themes of chivalry and glory. Gilded Rococo-style stucco carvings blaze across the palace's walls, and reach a garish intensity in the ballroom, where the Sciclunas' coat of arms – a white horse, representing purity and gallantry – stands proudly over a large mirror. After touring the house you can explore the garden, a green splash of lawns and fountains reminiscent of a British stately-home's garden; it also has an attractive conservatory of tropical plants such as palms and ferns.

Hotel

Corinthia Palace

De Paule Avenue, Balzan ⓣ25/440301, ⓦwww.corinthia.com. Sitting in manicured suburbs slap in the centre of Malta, the *Corinthia* offers a pleasant respite from the chaos of the resorts. Rooms are top-notch, and the classic flower-themed decor and amber colour scheme adds a touch of intimacy and homeliness; the spa offers a large range of high-tech treatments. Doubles €140, breakfast included.

Self-catering accommodation

University Residence

Triq Robert Mifsud Bonniċi, Lija ⓣ21/436168. Built for international students, these comfortable but basic three-bedroom apartments, rented on a sharing basis with communal kitchens and bathrooms, are a bargain. Facilities include swimming pool, tennis courts and Internet access. Note that no visitors are allowed after 11pm. Single bedroom €30.28; bed in a shared room (with two to four single beds) €11.65.

Shop

Ta Qali Crafts Village

Vjal L-Istadium Nazzjonali. Mon–Fri 9.30am–4.30pm, Sat 9.30am–12.30pm. Bus #80 from

▼ INTERIOR OF PALAZZO PARISIO

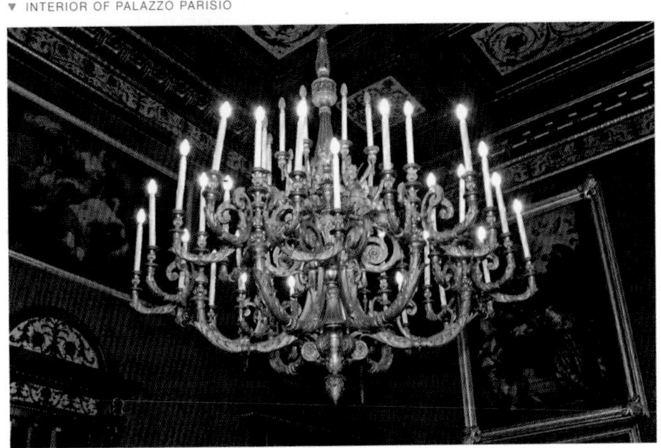

▲ GLASSBLOWING AT TA QALI CRAFTS VILLAGE

Valletta, #65 from Sliema, or #66 from Buġibba. Produced in the on-site workshops, the Maltese traditional crafts on sale – from blown glass and ceramics to jewellery, brassware and lace – are perfect if you're after an authentic and unusual souvenir.

Restaurants

Il-Melita Restaurant

Triq Birbal, Balzan ☎21/470663. Daily 10am–11pm. A large place adjacent to Sant Anton Gardens, this place serves an array of inexpensive meals such as pies, baguettes, pasta, pizza and even English breakfasts (served until 3pm), and more substantial Italian-style dinners from 7pm.

The Lord Nelson

278 Triq Il-Kbira, Mosta ☎21/432590. Tues–Sat 7.30–10pm. Closed for the week following New Year and the last three weeks of Aug. Despite the tables being too close together, the large 330-year-old townhouse decorated with traditional bric-a-brac makes an atmospheric setting. The menu – which changes three times yearly – features consistently good French- and Italian-style cuisine. Starters (around €8) might include chicken liver in brandy and cream served with rice, while mains (around €17) could be sea bass with roasted red peppers, anchovies, capers and lemon-infused oil.

Sarraċino's

Pjazza Tal-Knisja, Attard ☎21/422995. Daily: June–Sept 9am–2.30pm & 6pm–11pm; Oct–May 9am–10.30pm. Snacks such as *pastizzi*, salads and filled ciabatta, as well as pizza and pasta and dishes such as grilled salmon fillet (at €10.50 the most expensive item on the menu) are all served up in an old townhouse in the town square.

Bar

Żmerċ

Triq Birbal, Balzan ☎21/444576. Daily: Oct–May 10am–2.30pm & 6.30pm–2am; June–Sept 6.30pm–2am. Popular with young Maltese and students from the nearby *University Residence*, this lively bar is busiest in winter and is relatively undiscovered by tourists. Modestly priced drinks come with free tapas-style snacks, and there's blaring pop music as well as a big-screen TV for sports events. Traditional dinner feasts include horse meat, rabbit and fillet (evenings only for pre-booked groups; around €13 per person).

The northwest

Buġibba, a Seventies-style seaside resort, is the only densely populated place in a region otherwise characterized by a series of ridges and wide valleys, and two large bays that hold good sandy beaches. Despite the dearth of historical attractions, the northwest draws tourist traffic for its abundance of relatively inexpensive accommodation, particularly in Buġibba. Development becomes sparser further west in St Paul's Bay and Mellieħa, a pleasant, airy town with a distinctive feel that offers the best overall base in this part of Malta. The town's focal point is Mellieħa Bay, the island's largest beach, but the area also boasts some good restaurants and country walks. Transport connections are good for daytime touring but inadequate for regular night-time forays to other parts of the island.

Buġibba

Built up in the 1970s as a resort for sun-and-sea package tourism, Buġibba remains largely blighted by poor planning and hotchpotch development – the back-to-back apartment blocks and mid-range hotels are dense and dull. Cheap rents have attracted an increasing number of Maltese residents, and the inexpensive hotels continue to do brisk business, making Buġibba a viable, inexpensive base given

▲ BAY SQUARE, BUĠIBBA

Visiting the northwest

Direct services to Malta's main sights run from Buġibba's tourist-oriented bus station on Triq It-Turisti. Main routes are: #58 to Valletta; #48 to Ċirkewwa via St Paul's Bay and Mellieħa; #70 to Sliema; #652 to Għajn Tuffieħa and Golden Bay via St Paul's Bay; #86 to Rabat and Mdina; #427 to Marsaxlokk via Tarxien; and #627 to Sliema, the Three Cities and on to Marsaxlokk. All these services wind down by 9pm, and afterwards #49 operates between Paċeville (see p.76) and Buġibba until 1.30am.

All buses to Mellieħa pass through St Paul's Bay town centre and follow the coast road. Route #48 does the run between Buġibba and Ċirkewwa via Mellieħa; from Valletta, #44 terminates at Mellieħa Bay while #45 continues to Ċirkewwa, as does #652 from Sliema. All these buses bound for Ċirkewwa also pass Mellieħa Bay, Għadira Wetland, the Red Tower and Paradise Bay.

There are no night-time services to St Paul's Bay and Mellieħa.

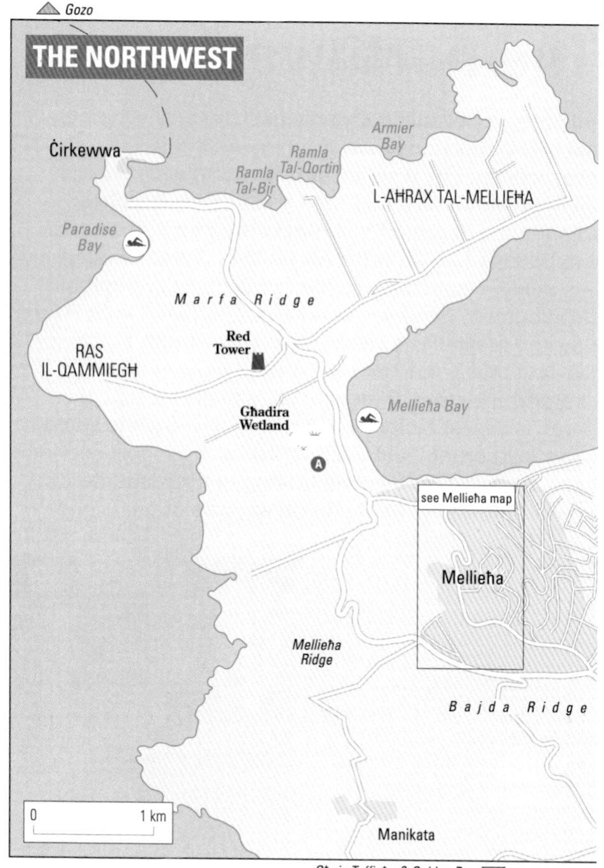

the good public transport connections. However, if you want to sample Malta's best in terms of sights, eating and drinking you'll find yourself spending the bulk of your time elsewhere.

The town's action is mostly concentrated in and around **Triq It-Turisti**, which is full of tour operators offering excursions round the islands and other tourist-oriented outlets, and the nearby **Bay Square** (Misraħ Il-Bajja), which is Buġibba's pedestrianized heart, a small plaza that's fringed by mediocre bars, restaurants and cafés.

The sea around the spit of land on which Buġibba is built isn't anything to write home about either, and the steep, rocky coast isn't nice or comfortable to lie on; your best bet is to head to one of the **lidos** that have sprouted up on the coast. The largest and best-equipped of these are Amazonia Beach Club (May–Oct 9am–6pm; €6 on weekdays, €12 at weekends), which has a pool, café and

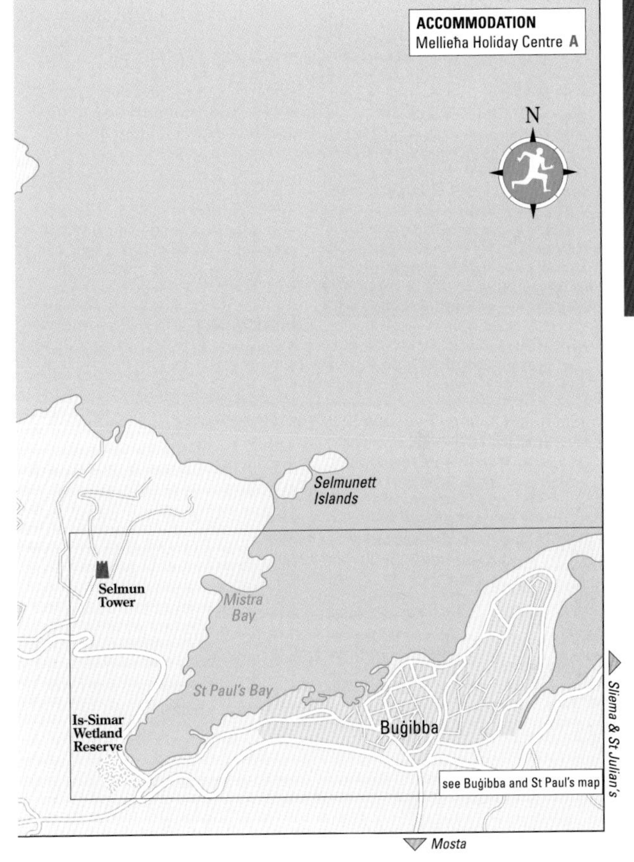

bar, and a nightclub that starts at 10pm; and the Sun and Surf in Salina Bay (May–Oct 9am–6pm; €8 on weekdays or €10.50 at weekends), with more space and more facilities.

St Paul's Bay

Buġibba meshes imperceptibly into St Paul's Bay, its ribbon of development skirting the coast towards the inner mouth of the bay itself and erupting into a mass of apartment blocks on the opposite side. Lying to the south of the Wignacourt Tower, and with a compact old centre of simple Baroque townhouses clustered around a small parish church, St Paul's Bay was originally a small fishing outpost, and though the small remaining fleet lends it a picturesque aspect, it's tourism that now holds sway – the town has a part-residential, part-resort feel. Yet with only a handful of bars and restaurants, St Paul's Bay is Buġibba's modest sister – minus the congestion and the touts – and provides a peaceful and

▲ ST PAUL'S BAY

more refined alternative to its neighbour's seaside tack.

Wignacourt Tower

Triq San Ġeraldu, St paul's Bay ☎21/215222. Mon–Wed, Fri & Sat 9.30am–12.30pm. €1.15. Built in 1609 to guard the entrance into St Paul's Bay, Wignacourt Tower is one of the largest of the defensive chain built around Malta's coastline by the Knights. A squarish, boxy design, its walls rising solidly to four partly embedded corner turrets, it now holds an interesting exhibition that illustrates the Knights' military architecture in Malta with prints of the designs and models of some of the varied defence structures scattered throughout the islands. The first floor, meanwhile, re-creates the living quarters of the *capomastro* (master bombardier), who was in charge of the tower with the assistance of two gunners. The soldiers led a plain, rather monastic life here, as evidenced by the undecorated bed, table and benches, and the stone cooking hearth. A staircase leads to the roof, where one of the two original cannons survive, and which affords a lovely view that takes in the entire sweep of St Paul's Bay.

Mistra Bay

There are no sandy beaches anywhere in the environs of St Paul's Bay, but the horseshoe-shaped Mistra Bay is a nice spot for a stroll by the sea. Scenically sitting at the mouth of a valley that steps up on either side to picturesque terraced fields, its shore consists of a strip of pebbles backed by the access road. The bay is a favourite place for anglers, and on its southern flank a path leads up from the shoreline to a bluff with trees and shrubs growing among heaps of boulders that tumble down to a clear sea; if you can negotiate getting in and out of the water here you'll be rewarded with good snorkelling among the rocky boulders that string the coast. If you walk to the end of the road that skirts around the bay and peters out at rugged cliffs, you'll get a lovely view

St Paul's shipwreck

The history of St Paul's Bay is firmly rooted in the story of the saint himself, who was shipwrecked here during his voyage to Rome to stand trial for heresy in 60 AD. St Paul quickly proved his miraculous abilities after he survived a snakebite – Maltese snakes, so the story goes, ceased to be venomous thereafter – and he then spent three months in Malta converting the population to Christianity. St Paul's story is now embedded in the Maltese national ethos; the date of the shipwreck, February 10, is a national holiday, and Paul is Malta's most revered saint, while the spot where he scrambled ashore, where Buġibba and St Paul's Bay meet, is commemorated by the small (and surprisingly uninteresting) St Paul's Shipwreck Church.

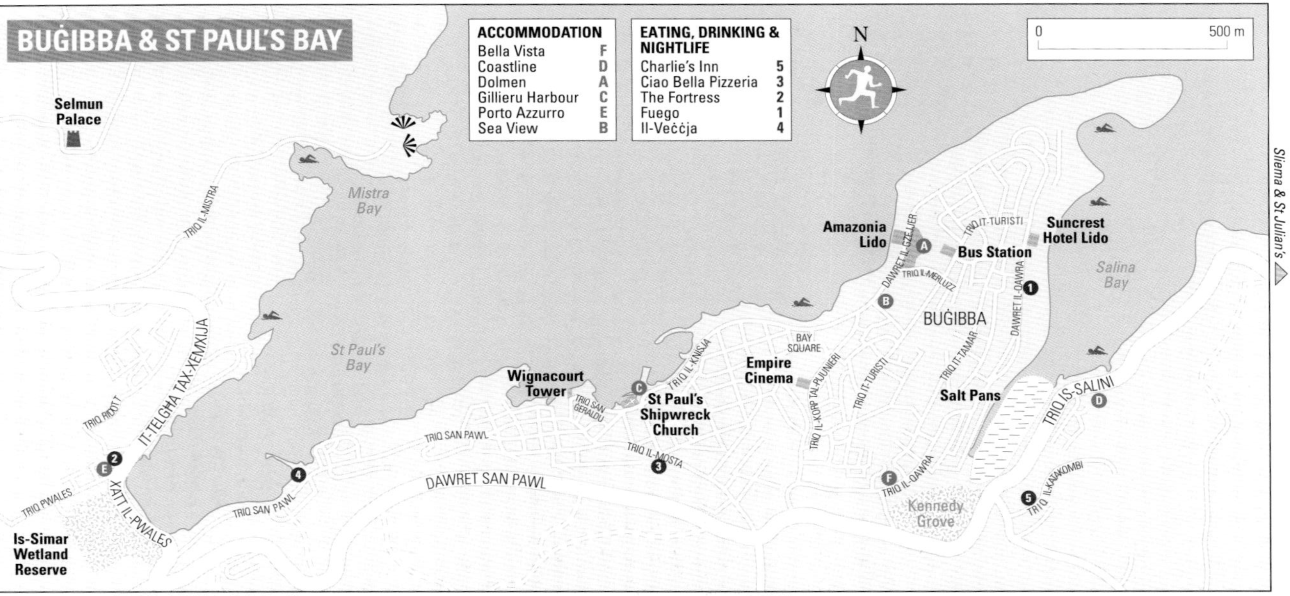
BUĠIBBA & ST PAUL'S BAY
ACCOMMODATION
Bella Vista F
Coastline D
Dolmen A
Gillieru Harbour C
Porto Azzurro E
Sea View B
EATING, DRINKING & NIGHTLIFE
Charlie's Inn 5
Ciao Bella Pizzeria 3
The Fortress 2
Fuego 1
Il-Veċċja 4
N
0
500 m
Selmun Palace
Mistra Bay
St Paul's Bay
Salina Bay
Amazonia Lido
Bus Station
Suncrest Hotel Lido
BUĠIBBA
BAY SQUARE
Empire Cinema
Wignacourt Tower
St Paul's Shipwreck Church
Salt Pans
Kennedy Grove
Is-Simar Wetland Reserve
TRIQ IL-MISTRA
IT-TELGĦA TAX-XEMXIJA
TRIQ RIDOTT
TRIQ PWALES
XATT IL-PWALES
TRIQ SAN PAWL
DAWRET SAN PAWL
TRIQ SAN GERALDU
TRIQ IL-MOSTA
TRIQ IL-KNISJA
TRIQ IL-KORP TAL-PIJUNIERI
TRIQ IT-TURISTI
TRIQ IL-QAWRA
TRIQ IT-TAMAR
DAWRET IL-GŻEJJER
TRIQ IL-MERLUZZ
DAWRET IL-QAWRA
TRIQ IS-SALINI
TRIQ IL-KATAKOMBI
Mellieħa
Sliema & St Julian's
Għajn Tuffieħa & Golden Bay
Mosta

▲ MISTRA BAY AND SELMUNETT ISLANDS

of **Selmunett Islands** (also known as St Paul's Islands), the two offshore isles where St Paul's galley supposedly smashed into the rocks. The largest of these isles – which are nature reserves designed to protect a sub-species of the Maltese lizard and Malta's last community of pure wild rabbits – has a large statue of St Paul trampling on a snake and brandishing the Bible; it was financed by a merchant in 1845.

At one place just left of the cliff's perch, the rocky coast peters out gently to meet the sea, providing access to the water in good weather – it's an excellent spot for snorkelling.

Mellieħa

Spread over the Mellieħa Ridge, Mellieħa has only recently developed any kind of a resort ethic, and the fringes of the largely anonymous residential sprawl have become peppered with a string of holiday apartments and exclusive villas that cling limpet-like to the slopes and cliffs, and spill down towards Mellieħa Bay.

The narrow, sloping Triq Ġorġ Borġ Olivier defines the town centre, and holds a smorgasbord of small shops and restaurants, including two great places to eat (see p.116 & 117).

At its northern extremity, Triq Ġorġ Borġ Olivier gives way to Triq Il-Marfa, the main artery that snakes down the slope to Mellieħa Bay, and then cuts across the Marfa Ridge all the way to Ċirkewwa (for the Gozo ferry).

▼ LIVING QUARTERS OF THE KNIGHTS, WIGNACOURT TOWER

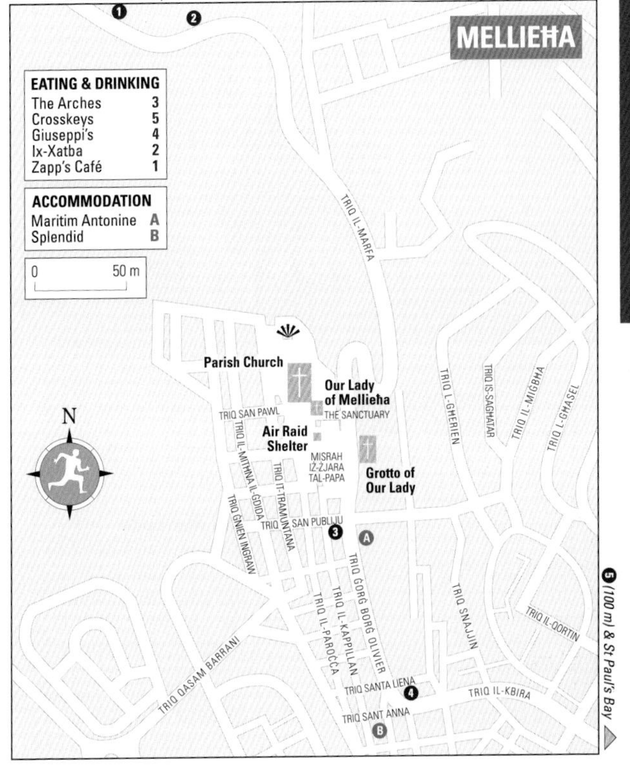

Mellieħa Church Complex

Misraħ Iż-Żjara Tal-Papa. Mellieħa's two churches are built on two levels at the edge of the Mellieħa Ridge, overlooking Mellieħa Bay. The Church of Our Lady of Mellieħa – the older of the two – is set in the **Sanctuary**, a lovely courtyard that's accessible from the square, Misraħ Iż-Żjara Tal-Papa, via the Monumental Arch, a Baroque stone archway built in 1716. The courtyard is flanked on the right by simple rooms built in the eighteenth century to house pilgrims, and on the left by the **Church of Our Lady of Mellieħa** (daily: June–Sept 8am–noon & 5–7pm; Oct–May 8am–noon & 4–6pm; free). An elegant structure embedded into the rockface, the church began as a crypt and has been expanded twice since the sixteenth century to accommodate the increasing number of pilgrims drawn to the fresco atop the altar, depicting the Madonna cradling Jesus in her arms and said to have been painted by St Luke in 60 AD. The clutter of votive offerings lining the tunnel into the church illustrate the continued belief in the fresco's healing powers, though recent studies have indicated that the saint may not have painted it. The church has a dimly lit

▲ SANCTUARY COURTYARD, MELLIEĦA

interior that's beautiful in its crude simplicity: the walls are panelled with marble, while the altar is framed by two marble columns and an arch topped by a crescent of gold-coloured mosaic.

Opposite the Monumental Arch, a second archway and staircase leads up to the bluff that the **Mellieħa Parish Church** (daily 6–8.30am & 5–7.30pm; free) stands on. Built in the mid-nineteenth century to accommodate the town's growing population, its lean pyramidal dome and bell towers, and its setting at the edge of the ridge, make it a dramatic feature of the skyline. The interior, however, is anti-climactic: a bare stone affair with only a few paintings, and a smattering of flowery Baroque motifs.

Grotto of Our Lady

Triq Ġorġ Borġ Olivier, Mellieħa. Daily 8am–6pm. Free. Across the road from the Sanctuary, a small unmarked doorway from Triq Ġorġ Borġ Olivier opens onto a staircase that cuts through an ivy-clogged little valley to the somewhat odd rock-cut chapel known as the Grotto of Our Lady, which has existed since medieval times. The only decoration under the slightly pitched roof is an unremarkable statue of the Madonna enclosed by a metal grille, with a pond

▲ FRESCO ALTARPIECE, CHURCH OF OUR LADY OF MELLIEĦA

fed by an underground spring at its foot; both are said to have miraculous healing powers. Many still have faith in the redemptive properties, as evidenced by the candles left by believers, and the votive offerings nailed to the walls.

Air Raid Shelter

Misraħ Iż-Żjara Tal-Papa, Mellieħa. Mon–Sat 9am–3.30pm. €2.30. Dug to protect Mellieħa's population during World War II air raids, the town's 500m of underground rooms and tunnels have now been opened up as a mildly diverting attraction about the use of the shelter during the war. Some of the rooms have been equipped with mannequins and furniture that re-create the way the shelters looked when in use, but the sound effects of children crying and bombs crashing that echo through the complex are unrealistic as Mellieħa was well outside the targets of the air raids. It's all rather dull and only worth visiting if you don't plan on going to the much more evocative similar exhibit in Vittoriosa (see p.64).

Mellieħa Bay

With almost 300m or so of sand lapped by water that stays ankle deep for some 50m out to sea, Mellieħa Bay is Malta's busiest beach, popular with tourists and Maltese families alike – it gets very crowded in summer. A main road runs parallel to the sand and there's plenty of parking, making it easily accessible. Its facilities add to the appeal, with watersport equipment, umbrellas and sun loungers for rent and several kiosks selling drinks and snacks.

▲ GROTTO OF OUR LADY, MELLIEĦA

Għadira Wetland

Mellieħa Bay ⓣ21/572603, ⓦwww.birdlifemalta.org. Nov–May Sat & Sun 10am–4pm. Free. This small, protected wetland serves as a point for water birds to rest and refuel during spring and autumn migration. There are two hides, equipped with binoculars and connected by a path; volunteers from Birdlife Malta guide you from one hide to the next, pointing out notable species along the way. It has a handful of resident birds, including moorhens and coots, and little ringed plovers. Although, overall the number of large water birds at any time is hit-and-miss, there are some notable regular species. Other winter residents include kingfishers, identifiable by their sharp trills as they fly low over the water, as well as many passerines, particularly warblers, robins and finches. The wild flowers also attract many colourful butterflies, and the reserve is home to chameleons, a fascinating creature you're almost guaranteed to see.

The Red Tower

Marfa Ridge ⓣ21/215222. June–Sept Mon–Thurs 10am–7pm & Fri–Sun 10am–4pm; Oct–May daily 10am–4pm. €1.15. Erected in 1649 and named for the dried-blood

▲ CHAMELEON AT GHADIRA WETLAND

colour of its paint job, the Red Tower cuts an imposing and rather fairy-tale figure on the Marfa Ridge, a rugged crest of garigue (a rocky habitat of herbaceous and hardy bushes) interspersed by groves of trees planted during a 1970s reforestation drive. The tower is a boxy construction with four mini-towers at each corner, and the Knights fitted it with cannons and stationed a brigade of 49 soldiers here, making it the main point of defence in this part of Malta. The British maintained its military role, using it as a signalling station during World War II. It's now been opened up to the public, kitted out with informative panels about the use and design of the tower, and you can also appreciate the interior's complex structure of arched buttresses and doorways designed to withstand cannon fire.

Ras Il-Qammiegħ

Marfa Ridge. Beyond the Red Tower, the narrow road that continues west along the crest of the ridge makes for an excellent walk or drive, with wonderful views on either side. Dotted with the stone huts of bird-trappers and hunters, the windswept, scrubby landscape is fragrant with wild thyme, whose light-purple flowers bloom in late spring (peaking in June). On the slopes on either side stand clumps of recently planted trees that are part of a reforestation drive. At the head of the ridge, the Ras Il-Qammiegh cliffs plummet down dramatically; at the base, boulders as large as churches tumble towards the sea. Facing south, you can see the craggy meander of the cliffs and inlets

▼ THE RED TOWER

that characterize the area's coastline; facing north, Comino and Gozo loom up from the shimmering sea. The alluring beach at the bottom of the immediate slope is Paradise Bay.

Paradise Bay

Ċirkewwa. This small stretch of sand snuggled into an inlet is the most attractive of all beaches on the Marfa Ridge peninsula, its creamy coloured sand interspersed with boulders and clumps of bamboo. The clear waters also offer some good snorkelling, and a bar serves refreshments and snacks. There's a car park on top of the bay, but if you're using public transport it's is a walk of 1km from the bus stop on the main road heading to Ċirkewwa.

Hotels

Bella Vista

Triq Il-Qawra, Buġibba ⓣ21/570591, ⓦwww.bellavista.com.mt. This small hotel on the fringes of town has limited facilities, a buffet-style restaurant, a small bar and a pool boxed-in by high walls, but the spacious en-suite rooms, with plain pine furniture, small TVs and phones, are hard to beat at this price. Doubles €65, breakfast included.

Coastline

Triq Is-Salini, Buġibba ⓣ21/573781, ⓦwww.islandhotels.com. Large, imposing hotel, with a stepped, pyramidal profile, that's set back from the main coast road on the outskirts of Buġibba. The grounds are spacious, and the massive lobby and long corridors lead to large, comfortable, pastel-coloured en-suite rooms that have a/c and phones. Doubles €125, breakfast included.

Dolmen

Triq Dolmen, Buġibba ⓣ21/581510, ⓦwww.dolmen.com.mt. Right on the coast, this large hotel is something of a Buġibba institution, with a casino and a great fusion restaurant. The exterior is imposing and tasteless and the interior garish, but the huge range of facilities include a nightclub, two pools, a private lido and watersports; the comfortable en-suite rooms have all modern conveniences. Doubles from €105, breakfast included.

Gillieru Harbour

Triq Il-Knisja, Buġibba ⓣ21/572720, ⓦwww.gillieru.com. Attractive hotel overlooking Selmunett Islands, with circular balconies and wrought-iron balustrades. The cream-coloured en-suite rooms are cheerful and have a/c, phones and TVs, while the restaurant cooks up good seafood dishes. Doubles €90, breakfast included.

Maritim Antonine

Triq Ġorġ Borġ Olivier, Mellieħa ⓣ21/520923, ⓦwww.maritim.com.mt. An attractive cream-and-maroon building in Mellieħa town centre, with an equally swanky interior. Facilities include a swimming pool in the lush gardens and some spa facilities, while the rooms are spacious, with TVs, phones, a/c and luxurious en-suite bathroom. €150 for doubles, breakfast included.

Porto Azzurro

Triq Ridott, St Paul's Bay ⓣ21/585171, ⓦwww.portoazzurro.com.mt. Modern, functional and attractive mauve-painted hotel offering 25 cheerful en-suite rooms with a/c, and dozens of self-contained apartments (studios and one-bedroom) with ceiling fans. Doubles €75 including breakfast; apartments from €60.

Sea View

Triq Il-Qawra, Buġibba ⓣ21/573105, ⓦwww.seaviewhotelmalta.com. This small, family-run property near the sea in the centre of Buġibba is ideal as a cheap base. The 49 rooms lack flair but are functional; each has a small toilet and shower or bath, fan and TV, and you can get a fridge on request for an extra €2.30 per day. They also have a family room and some singles. Doubles €42, breakfast included.

Guesthouse

Splendid

Triq P.P. Magri, Mellieħa ⓣ21/523602, ⓦwww.splendidmalta.com. Attractive townhouse in the heart of Mellieħa offering ten basic double rooms (some with three or four single beds). All have fans, but you can pay €4.50 per day for a/c, and most have their own shower and sink, and share toilets – an extra €4.50 daily upgrades you to a fully en-suite room. Doubles €40.

Apartments

Mellieħa Holiday Centre

Mellieħa Bay ⓣ22/893000, ⓦwww.mhc.com.mt. Set in neatly landscaped grounds of tamarisk trees and palms, these 150 cheery bungalows have kitchens and terraces fronting the gardens; thirty of them also have a/c. All have two bedrooms, and can sleep up to six. The Danish restaurant is reliable, and there's a supermarket on site. From €87 for two, breakfast included.

Restaurants

The Arches

Triq Ġorġ Borġ Olivier, Mellieħa ⓣ21/520533. Mon–Sat 7–10.30pm. Funky modern decor with classic touches and French-inspired fusion dishes. The imaginative menu changes seasonally, and may include pasta with prawns, ham, lobster, cream and dill (€11) or mains such as guinea fowl cooked in lemon, fennel and port wine (€16).

Charlie's Inn

Triq Il-Katakombi, Buġibba ⓣ21/573455. June–Oct Mon–Sat 7–11pm; Nov–May Tues–Sat 7–11pm & Sun noon–3pm. Traditional rabbit dishes are famous in Malta, and this is the best place to find out what the fuss is about. Rabbit is cooked in four different ways (all around €15): simmered in garlic and white wine; stewed with tomato sauce and peas; baked with tomatoes and red wine; or barbecued and served with gravy. They only cook to order, which can mean a long wait for your meal.

Ciao Bella Pizzeria

Triq Il-Mosta, St Paul's Bay ⓣ21/580112. Tues–Sun 6.30–11pm, plus Sun noon–2.30pm. Informal place offering pizzas (€4.50–7), ranging from the simple topped with tomatoes, mozzarella and Parma ham, to the more elaborate Pizza Contadina, with mozzarella, bacon, mushrooms, onions, green pepper and blue cheese. They also do grilled meats and fish and standard Italian pasta, all for around €9.

Giuseppi's

Triq Ġorġ Borġ Olivier, Mellieħa ⓣ21/574882. Tues–Sat 7.30–10.30pm.

▲ GIUSEPPI'S

This converted townhouse full of intriguing bric-a-brac makes a great setting for some of Malta's best cooking. The regularly changing menu includes daily fish-based specialities, and traditional dishes prepared with a twist, such as rabbit with chocolate. Favourites include grilled calamari with herb sauce, and linguini with sea urchins. Around €15 for main courses.

Il-Veċċja

Triq San Pawl, St Paul's Bay ☎21/575416. April–Oct daily 7–10.30pm; Nov–March Mon & Wed–Sun 7–10pm. Small, cosy restaurant set in an old building, which serves creative Italian dishes, ranging from simple fish grilled on charcoal, to more elaborate choices like risotto with lobster (€8.15) or chicken breast with Parma ham cooked in cider and apple sauce (€11).

Ix-Xatba

Triq Il-Marfa, Mellieħa ☎21/521753. June–Oct daily 6–10.30pm; mid-Nov–May Mon & Wed–Sun 6–10.30pm. Closed for one month mid-Jan to mid-Feb, and two weeks in Nov. Unassuming but consistently creative all-rounder offering standard Italian risottos and pastas, mostly featuring fish or shellfish, as well as many seafood mains. There are also eight types of fillet steaks, and lamb baked with herbs; the menu is rounded off with traditional dishes such as rabbit, ravioli, *pulpetti* (spicy fried meatballs) and *bragioli* (baked beef wrapped around a meat stuffing). Around €13 for main courses.

Bars and cafés

Crosskeys

Misraħ Tas-Salib, Mellieħa ☎21/522605. Daily 11.30am–1am. Popular with locals and tourists alike, the busiest pub in town has cosy wooden decor and a playlist of varied commercial music. British-style roasts are available on Sundays.

The Fortress

Triq It-Telgħa Tax-Xemxija, St Paul's Bay ☎21/579852. April–Oct daily 7.30–11.30pm; Nov–May Tues–Sun

▲ OUTDOOR DINERS, BUĠIBBA

7–11pm (call in advance in winter as it closes early if quiet). Malta's finest wine bar is set in an old fortress, with Baroque tables and fixtures inside and plush canopies and tables outside on a large terrace. The music is a tasteful selection of chilled-out dance tunes, the wine list is massive (prices start from €10), and the platters of finger food are good, especially the themed selections such as Asian, Maltese and Italian (prices start at €9 for two sharing).

Joseph Bar

Mellieħa Holiday Centre, Mellieħa Bay ⓣ22/893000. Daily 10am–12.30am. The large poolside café of this holiday resort is comfortable, chic and nicely decorated in warm colours. Coffee, tea, cakes and snacks are served, as is alcohol, and there's live music every evening – mostly rock, as well as blues and jazz.

Zapp's Café

Triq Il-Marfa, Mellieħa ⓣ21/576415. Daily 11am–1am (later in summer). Friendly local drifters' hangout, with a TV screen often tuned into football matches from European leagues. They also serve tasty quick bites such as rolls and pies, and a large range of relatively cheap pizzas.

Club

Fuego

Dawret Il-Qawra, Buġibba ⓣ21/584933, ⓦwww.fuego.com.mt. Daily 10.30pm–4am. The sister operation of the successful Paċeville outfit (see p.82) is Buġibba's most popular club, with beach bar-style decor, plenty of potted palms and bamboo, South American cocktails and commercial Latin music.

The southeast

Malta's least-touristy region consists of a clutch of old towns that have retained a measure of quaint town life that has disappeared in the more commercial north. Most distinct is Żejtun, a self-possessed old-style town whose charm, aside from its outstanding church, comes from its atmosphere; wandering the streets, which are full of intricate architectural motifs, makes you feel like you've escaped all the tourists to Malta. More famous is Marsaxlokk, a fishermen's town whose bay is full of traditional fishing boats and a couple of good seafood restaurants. The region is also home to Malta's finest four Neolithic temples, all World Heritage Sites and all subtly different – ranging from the underground Hypogeum near Tarxien to two temples set in a spectacular landscape of tumbling coastal cliffs near Wied Iż-Żurrieq.

Tarxien Neolithic temples

Triq It-Tempji Neolitiċi, Tarxien ⓣ21/695578, ⓦwww.heritagemalta.org. Daily 9am–5pm. €2.33. Buses #11, #12, #13 from Valletta, #427 from Buġibba, and #627 or #427 from Marsaxlokk. The largest and most architecturally advanced temple complex in Malta, Tarxien's Neolithic temples were among the last batch built on the island, constructed between 3000 and 2500 BC. Evidence of fires here suggests that Bronze Age peoples used the buildings as a crematorium, but thereafter the complex lay buried under an accumulation of rubble until it was discovered by a farmer in 1914, when he investigated the large rocks that kept ruining his plough. What survives now is the bottom third of the temples, although that's still relatively impressive considering that the building, when intact, stood some 23m high.

Although the temple is now surrounded and dwarfed by buildings, it's a good place to start a tour of the four Neolithic temples covered in this chapter. The complex comprises three interlinked temples, and entry

Visiting the southeast

As the attractions in the southeast are fairly scattered, travelling to them mostly entails doubling back to Valletta to catch buses to the far-flung sights. However, there are two specialized bus routes that serve the main tourist circuit in the region. The most useful of these is #627 which starts at Buġibba, runs via St Julian's and Sliema, and then calls at the Three Cities (see p.64) and Marsaxlokk before looping back – via Tarxien – towards Sliema, St Julian's and the Buġibba terminal. The #427 also starts from Buġibba in a round journey that covers Mosta and Attard (see p.99), Tarxien and Marsaxlokk. Żejtun, and Birżebbuġa, in the Żurrieq region, are reachable on separate routes from Valletta.

is through the massive trilithons of the **South Temple**; the first chamber holds a grand altar with spiral reliefs, and a replica of the bottom half of the "fat lady" figure found here (the original resides in Valletta's Archeology Museum; see p.52); when whole, it would have measured 2.5m high, making it the largest of these figures found anywhere in the world. From here, a passageway leads to the expansive **Middle Temple**, with its three pairs of small, symmetrical chambers. The inner two have knee-high slate-thin stone frames, smothered with spiral whorls and wedged into the passageway, and thought to mark the threshold into the temple's inner sanctum. If you look closely at a chamber to the right, you can see faded motifs of marching bulls and goats carved on the megaliths.

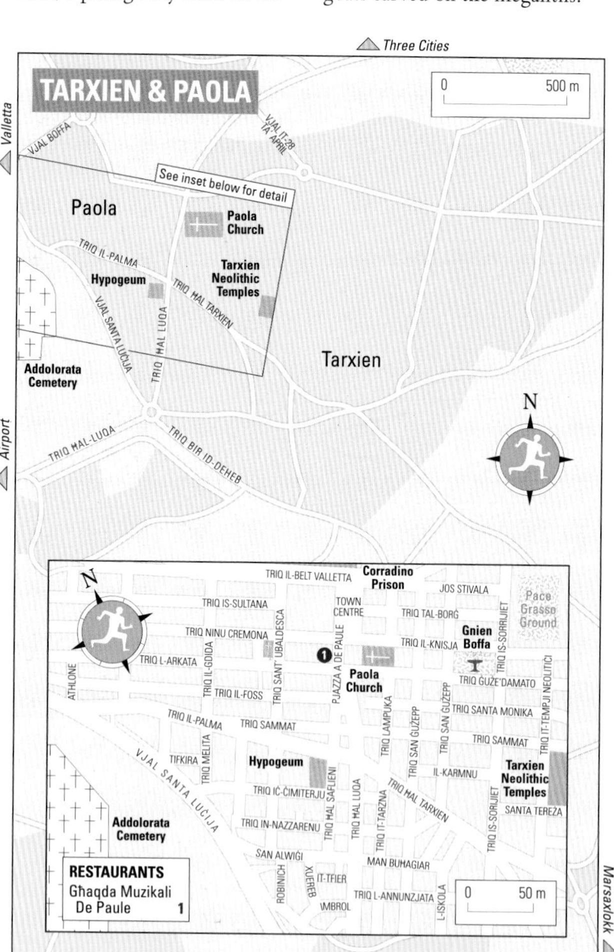

▲ TARXIEN TEMPLES

The Middle Temple leads to the **East Temple**, of which only the bottom foundation stones survive.

The Hypogeum

Triq Ic-Ċimiterju, Paola ⓣ21/805019, ⓦwww.heritagemalta.org. Daily 9am–5pm. €9.32. Bus #11, #12, #13 from Valletta, #427 from Buġibba, and #627 or #427 from Marsaxlokk.

An extensive underground shrine spread over three levels, two of which are open to the public, the Hypogeum is one of the oldest and most impressive monuments of the ancient world. Built between 3600 and 2500 BC, it was still a work in progress when Malta's Neolithic settlers disappeared without trace, and was only rediscovered in 1899. Subsequent excavations yielded the remains of 7000 bodies, as well as artefacts such as stone mallets, green stone necklaces and the famous "sleeping lady" figure (see p.52).

The full purpose of the Hypogeum remains a matter of conjecture and debate; archeologists are now seeing its function as wider than that of a simple necropolis. It was certainly connected to the role of death in the larger scheme of life, but the fact that only 7000 bodies have been recovered – which means just seven burials per year over the thousand years the Hypogeum was in use – suggests that only

Visiting the Hypogeum

As only seventy people are allowed into the Hypogeum each day to ensure its preservation, visits need to be planned well ahead – bookings are often filled solid for a couple of weeks in advance in the summer, and your only chance of getting in at the last minute is either if someone cancels or if you manage to get on the expensive noon tour. You can book tickets at the Hypogeum itself, at the National Museum of Archeology in Valletta (see p.52), or in Gozo at the Ġgantija Temples (see p.143) or Archeology Museum (see p.137). But your best bet is online at ⓦwww.heritagemaltashop.com before you arrive in Malta. If all else fails, you might still get on the special daily tour at noon – this is left open for visitors to turn up on the day, and it can't be booked; instead, a group of ten is assembled on a first-come basis; the catch is that this tour costs €20.

▲ BOWL FROM THE HYPOGEUM

shamans, priests or priestesses were laid here for eternal or temporary rest. Intriguingly, some rooms were designed to look like the inside chambers of temples, something that gives you an insight into how above-ground temples would have looked when intact. But whatever the Hypogeum's exact function, it's a unique structure with a tangible air of mystery, and you really do have to see it to appreciate its profoundly stirring atmosphere.

The 45-minute tours of the complex start with a short video, then you use an audio-guide to see the first and second levels – lights are synchronized with the audio guide, coming on and off automatically in different rooms to lead you on. The guide starts at the jumble of ruins on the **first level**, hacked out long ago, that highlight the intact entrance trilithon – two upright megaliths with another laid on top to make a gateway into the underground realm. The **second level**, daubed with representations of the spiral in red ochre (perhaps representing the Neolithic people's world-view of cyclical continuity), has lobed chambers that served as graves, and an incomplete section that illustrates how the complex was dug out, generation after generation, by first boring holes with deer antlers, then knocking off chunks of rock between the cavities with stone mallets, and finally polishing the walls. Further on, the **Oracle Room** is decorated by a faint painted tree thought to symbolize the tree of life; the room itself takes its name from the Oracle Hole, an opening in the wall which, when spoken into, amplifies a baritone voice into an echo that booms through the underground space.

Beyond this lies the heart of the complex: two interconnected chambers known as the **Holy of Holies** and the **Main Chamber**, dug out to suggest walls of megaliths (as though you're standing inside an above-ground temple), and used for ceremonies that remain a mystery.

Addolorata Cemetery

Triq Il-Labour, Marsa. Daily 7am–5pm. Free. Buses #1, #2, #4 or #6 from Valletta. Consecrated in 1869 and ranged up a hillside, Malta's largest burial ground is worth exploring for its Gothic Revival architecture, lush landscaping, and large collection of bombastic Baroque tombs. From the entrance, a path meanders uphill past elaborate marble-cased tombstones overhung by cypress, olives, carobs and Aleppo pines. Each tombstone is unique, created by the family who own it, and the hotchpotch of designs, statues and motifs is bewildering; additionally, at the higher reaches of the cemetery the well-to-do are laid to rest inside sumptuous Neoclassical and Baroque mausoleums. The Gothic Revival chapel at the top of the hill is closed to the public, but the ornate exterior is worth admiring, with a facade that tapers to a pointed pinnacle, punctuated by attractive stained-glass windows.

Żejtun

Bus #27 from Valletta or the bus stop outside Tarxien Neolithic temples.

The old town of Żejtun is

Neolithic Malta

Malta's Neolithic community, which blossomed from 5000–2500 BC, was the most advanced civilization of its time: the temples are the oldest free-standing man-made structures in the world and the relics within are more artistically sophisticated than anything found elsewhere of the same period. Almost 25 major temples have been discovered in Malta so far, and this fact has presented archeologists with intractable puzzles.

The islands are thought to have supported between 5000 and 10,000 inhabitants, and the mobilization required to build the megalithic temples would mean that many of these inhabitants had to be working on them. This seems strange and unlikely for the simple reason that the inhabitants also had to produce their food, and maintain their private dwellings. Generations of archeologists have pored over this contradiction, which is complicated by the fact that in around 2500 BC the Neolithic community came to an inexplicable and sudden end.

The most mainstream theory is that the inhabitants over-exploited the environment, and as their natural resources dwindled, they became obsessed with fertility and religious salvation from their predicament. This led them to devote all their resources to building the temples, something that eventually hastened their end in the form of environmental collapse. Critics of this theory argue that there is no supporting evidence whatsoever about environmental denudation, and the temple people would have documented this, or left some sign of it; by contrast, the erection of the temples is in itself a sign that the people had abundant resources – because people turn to art only once their basic food necessities are secured.

Another theory that has attracted more publicity in recent years holds that Malta at the time was much larger, and what survives is the tip of its mountain, on which most of the temples are concentrated. There is geological plausibility in this: the Pantelleria Rift, southwest of Malta, where the African and European continental plates crunch into each other, constantly produces upwarping of the land, and this could have led to a massive earthquake that destroyed the larger part of Malta, and its inhabitants. Circumstantial evidence for this theory is the fact that the southwest–northeast tilt of the islands is increasing, and the sheer clear-cut cliffs that girdle the entire southern coasts appear to have been formed by a violent earthquake – yet there is no hard proof for this or any other theory – and the studies and arguments continue unabated.

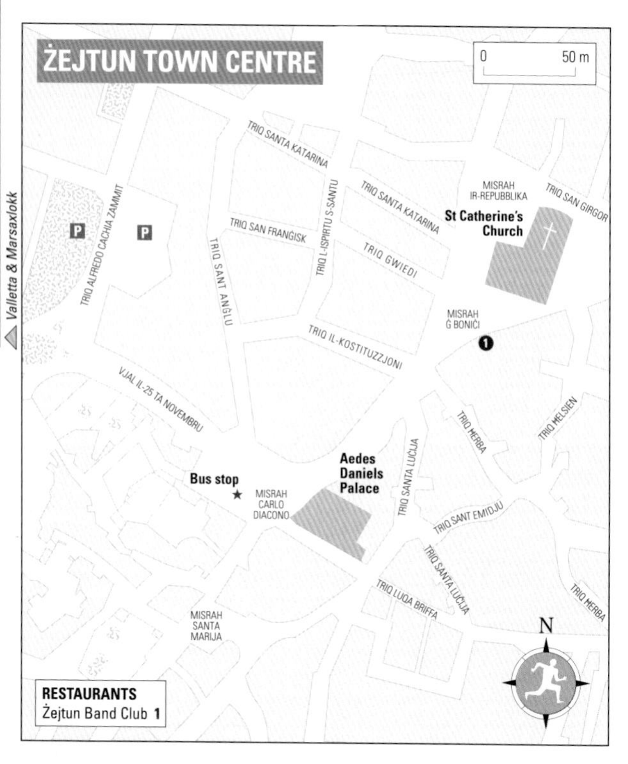

largely and unjustifiably off the tourist trail; this makes it all the more pleasant to stroll along its quiet sun-dappled streets to take in the mighty church, ornate Baroque buildings, and quaint town life. The town has a long history: it has prospered since Phoenician times, and its name, Żejtun – meaning olive in Arabic – suggests that the area was probably involved in production of olive oil. Later, Żejtun was one of the twelve independent parishes that were established by 1436. Detritus from all these periods is scattered through the town, although the central focus of a visit is the massive **St Catherine's Church**, which dominates the skyline for miles around. Designed by Lorenzo Gafa in 1692 in his distinctive style, its setting and structure is impressive, and its interior (open for Mass Mon–Sat 6–8.15am & 4.30–7pm, Sun 6–11.45am & 5–6pm; free) has three excellent paintings in the chancel that depict St Catherine's martyrdom. The central one, painted by students of Mattia Preti, shows the saint surrounded by soldiers and rulers in a dark, momentous mood; the other two paintings on either side of the chancel, which are the works of the Maltese artist Francesco Zahra (1710–73), are equally dramatic, showing the court convicting Catherine and angels carrying her headless body to heaven.

▲ ORNATE DOORWAY IN ŻEJTUN

On a different note, the side-altar to the right of the chancel has an outstanding medieval painting of the Madonna holding baby Jesus on her lap rendered on wood.

Outside the church the streets are littered with medieval architectural features. The most distinctive building, situated near the bus station on Misraħ Carlo Diacono, is **Aedes Daniels Palace**, which was once the home of Girgor Bonici (1612–97), who served as a mayor of Mdina. The imposing facade features a large statue of an Old Testament prophet set in a niche mounted on two lions, and adorned by three heads of ghoulish human-looking animals; next to the building are two medieval chapels. Along the southern flank of Aedes Daniels is Triq Luqa Briffa, which leads east to the town's old quarter, starting at Triq Ħerba on the left, with a maze of twisty alleyways, old buildings, niches of saints and other delightful architectural details. Heading north will eventually bring you back to the church square.

Ħal Millieri Chapel of the Annunciation

Ħal Millieri ☎21/215222. Open first Sun of every month 9am–noon. Free. Bus #38 or #138 from Valletta.

Unfortunately open only one morning a month, the small cuboid chapel of Ħal Millieri – which is hidden behind a walled garden of cypress and palm trees where plague victims were once buried – holds a

▼ ST CATHERINE'S CHURCH, ŻEJTUN

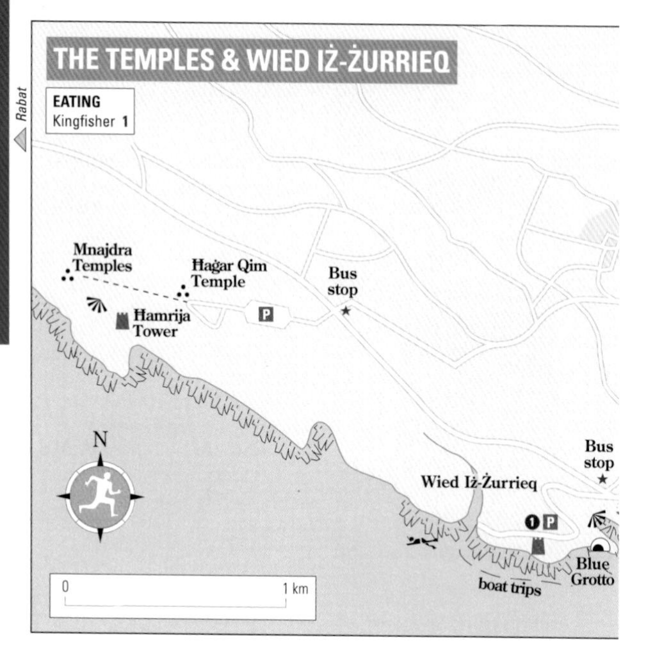

fantastic set of medieval frescoes. The chapel, which was erected in 1450 and is the only building left standing of the former hamlet of Ħal Millieri, is itself an outstanding example of advanced medieval architecture with its pitched roof held up by interior stone arches. Yet it's the frescoes, which were found under several layers of paint during a restoration project, that steal the show. Dating from the fifteenth century, they depict the venerated saints of the time, some brandishing bibles, and one riding a horse. The style of the paintings is Byzantine, and the saints are dressed in colourful vestments and ceremonial hats in a range of pastel colours made from natural dyes. The colours have survived for so long only because they were protected under layers of waterpaint, and the chapel is now only open once a month to help preserve them: too much carbon dioxide produced by human visitors would quickly damage the

▼ FRESCOES IN ĦAL MILLIERI CHAPEL

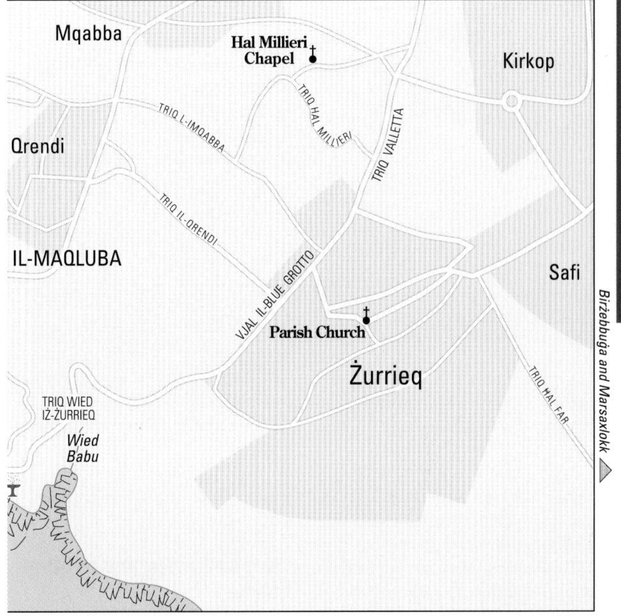

colours. It's also open for the feast which falls on the first Sunday after March 25 (8.30am–6.30pm), when a mass with choir takes place at 10am. To find the chapel, once you reach Żurrieq, on Triq Valletta, take the first right beyond the petrol station, and then turn right again about 1km down the road.

Ħaġar Qim and Mnajdra Neolithic temples

Triq Ħaġar Qim ⓦwww.heritagemalta.org. Daily 9am–5pm. €4.66 per temple or €7 for combined ticket, but due to rise in 2008. Bus #32, #38 or #138 from Valletta. The Ħaġar Qim and Mnajdra Neolithic temple complexes are Malta's most atmospheric temples, situated on a rugged and scenic rocky plateau that reaches down to the area's dramatic cliffs – a windswept setting, scented by thyme that grows in the rocky habitat, that's pretty much unchanged since the time when the structures were built. Built within 1km of each other, both were constructed and used between 3600 and 2500 BC, and they still make a stirring sight, despite the transparent protective shields that were put up in 2008 to protect them from weather-induced erosion. The new visitors' centre being erected at the time of writing will document the construction and use of the temples.

The first temple, **Ħaġar Qim**, is the least understood of all Maltese temples. Uniquely, it is a circular complex consisting of four temples with two opposite entrances – the one nearest the gate, through which you enter, and a back entrance along the passage that bisects the whole structure. Set on the plateau's crest, the

▲ ĦAĠAR QIM TEMPLE

temple is now semi-ruined, but would originally have been an imposing edifice; the heavy facade and the large upright megaliths that survive give you an idea of its former grandeur. Its design departs from the paired-apses template of Malta's other temples: the spaces and chambers open into each other in an intricate jumble of rooms, and the understanding of these spatial arrangements, and their ceremonial significance, is close to nil. Among the fertility relics unearthed here – now at the National Museum of Archeology in Valletta (see p.52) – are a "fat lady" figurine and three phallus sculptures.

A five-minute walk along a gently inclining path brings you to the **Mnajdra** complex, which consists of three temples that form a continuous concave facade – the arena-like space within is thought to have been a place where the common people could congregate whilst priests or priestesses conducted ceremonies inside. The East Temple is the smallest and most primitive of the three, and only its foundations survive, while the bare Middle Temple has twin entrances at the front, as well as an architectural plan of its facade, carved into the left passageway megalith at the time of construction (and claimed to be the first-ever architectural design). The elegant South Temple is the best preserved of any on the Maltese islands. Its two pairs of chambers, with symmetrical apses, are small and intimate; beyond them, the inner lobe and sanctum has three of its altars propped on round tapered stones. The so-called Oracle Hole, in the first chamber on the right, is a small aperture that opens into a hidden cubicle that's thought to have been the seat of a hidden oracle who perhaps passed on messages or mantras, or interpreted epiphanies during ceremonies.

Wied Iż-Żurrieq and the Blue Grotto

Bus #38 or #138 from Valletta.

Enclosed by a deep gorge and lying at the mouth of a creek, the former fishing outpost of **Wied Iż-Żurrieq** has grown into a mini-resort, with a few restaurants and souvenir shops flanking the creek. The village's boathouses are fronted by a small exposed garden of wind-tufted tamarisks, which affords good sea views; the garden itself is dominated by the seventeenth-century tower that served as one of the chain of coastal defences (it now houses the local police station). Some 6km offshore from the settlement is the tiny islet of Filfla, a nature reserve that's off limits to the public so as to protect its large colony of secretive storm petrel birds. Most people come to Wied Iż-Żurrieq to board one of the boats that ferry some 100,000 visitors each year on the fifteen-minute excursions

▲ KNIGHTS' TOWER AT WIED IŻ-ŻURRIEQ

(daily 9am–5pm; €7) to the Blue Grotto and other smaller caves. **The Blue Grotto** is a dramatic spot – the huge domed cave opening at sea level is fronted by a buttress eroded into the rocks, and the sea within has a deep-blue luminosity – but the constant boat-traffic ruins the atmosphere and leaves a noxious pall of engine exhaust. If you don't fancy joining the camera-toting packs that crowd the boats, you can find an excellent high-point view of the cave by peering down the cliff at a public garden where the side-road climbing from Wied Iż-Żurrieq joins the main road at the crossroads.

Marsaxlokk

Bus #27 from Valletta, #427 from Buġibba, or #627 from Sliema.

Set around the deep scoop of Marsaxlokk Bay, Marsaxlokk is home port for Malta's largest fishing fleet, and the spectacle of the town's fishermen and their painted wooden boats remains its principal allure. The town's harbour is a colourful riot of *luzzu* boats – the eyes painted on their prows are supposed to lead fishermen to their catch. Demanding great skill to build, *luzzu* are more expensive now than modern fibreglass boats, but most fishermen prefer them for their sturdiness, stability and durability. The fishermen are small-scale and their fishing methods are quaint and traditional; you can see them onshore mending nets, preparing for fishing trips, or, in winter, painting their boats. The activity reaches its zenith

▼ MNAJDRA TEMPLE

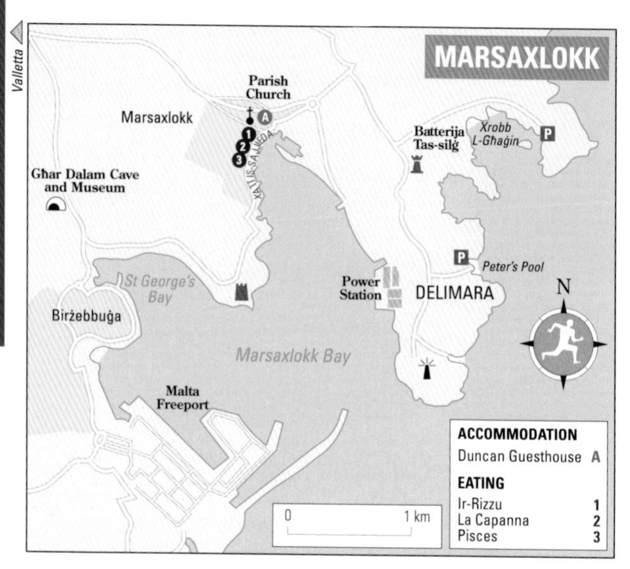

during the fishing season for *lampuki* (dolphin fish), Malta's most popular fish, which is caught when it migrates to the Mediterranean to spawn during the late summer and autumn.

The town's seafront promenade serves as its centre, with the church and small pedestrianized square set by the shore. On either side of the square lie a string of restaurants, social clubs and cafés; opposite the church, hawkers sell souvenirs, clothes and fresh fish. A couple of restaurants cook delectable and fresh seafood (see p.132), and the tables set on the water's edge during warm weather make a great spot for a romantic dinner.

Delimara beaches

Enclosing Marsaxlokk Bay to the east and forming the southeastern tip of Malta, the Delimara promontory is mostly comprised of agricultural fields and bird-trapping sites set among groves of Aleppo pines. The main reason to visit is the two scenic bays gouged into Delimara's seaward flank; their shore is sculpted into a combination of dramatic cliff-faces, rocky pinnacles, and plateaux that peter out at the water's edge. The water offshore is an ideal spot for swimming or snorkelling but the limestone shores aren't comfortable for sunbathing. You have to jump into the water, and when the wind is blowing in it tends to wash in unsightly flotsam; visit on a day when the wind is blowing from northern or westerly directions, or when it's dead calm. Best of the two bays, in terms of swimming, is **Peter's Pool**; the other bay, **Xrobb L-Għġin** (or Island Bay), is cut in more scenic chalky cliffs, but it also serves as the shore hub for a large fish-farm offshore, and the boats coming and going impinge on the atmosphere. You'll either need your own transport to get to Delimara or it's a thirty-minute walk from Marsaxlokk;

once the single-access road climbs to the promontory, take the right fork for Peter's Pool (then watch out for the sign or you'll miss the dirt track to the bay; there is a car park backing the bay), or the left fork for Xrobb L-Għġin.

Għar Dalam Cave and Museum

Triq Iż-Żejtun, Birżebbuġa ⓣ21/657419, ⓦwww.heritagemalta.org. Daily 9am–5pm. €3.50. Bus #11, #12 or #13 from Valletta. Although billed as a major sight, and a stopover on most tour operators' circuits, Għar Dalam Cave and Museum holds scant appeal for general visitors, unless you've got a scholarly interest in Malta's ancient past or in paleontology. The cave is significant as it's considered to be the place where Malta's human story began, but the exhibits themselves are mostly limited to bones and reconstructed animal skeletons. Excavations of the 145-metre-deep cave, which were mostly carried out following its discovery in 1892, yielded human teeth and a skull that were dated to 7000 years ago, making them the island's earliest human remains (one author has claimed that the tests where misconstrued, and that the teeth are actually 12,000 years old, an assertion that some archeologists have preliminarily supported and no one has rebuffed). Other detritus found within includes shreds of pottery, rodents'-teeth necklaces, and the remains of prehistoric animals flushed into the cave at the end of the last Ice Age. Before and during the Ice Age, the level of the Mediterranean Sea fluctuated between 30m and 200m lower than it is today, and Malta was intermittently connected to continental Europe via land bridges. Animals retreated south to escape the cold, and their carcasses drifted down ancient rivers to be deposited here – the 125,000-year-old remains unearthed include hippopotamus and dwarf elephant. There were also large European mammals, who found themselves marooned in Malta when the ice thawed and the sea level rose, and, with limited territory and food these animals' growth was

▼ DELIMARA

stunted – the femurs of red deer, for example, are half the size of their European counterparts. All these relics are now exhibited in the small museum adjoining the cave, which is also open to visitors.

Guesthouse

Duncan Guesthouse

32 Xatt Is-Sajjieda, Marsaxlokk ☎21/657212, Ⓦwww.duncanmalta.com. Marsaxlokk's only accommodation option, adjacent to the church, has ten studio apartments – twins, doubles and some with four single beds – all self-contained rooms with bathrooms. Although spartan, the rooms feature new pine furniture, including dressers and dining tables, as well as a fridge, coffee machine, toaster, sink, a/c and TV (visitors who stay for a week or more can also request a cooker and use the laundry room). Doubles and twins €41, €23.50 for single occupancy; four-person rooms €60.

Restaurants

Għaqda Muzikali De Paule

Pjazza De Paule, Paola ☎21/805431. Daily 8am–midnight. The café of the local brass-band club offers palatable meals at rock-bottom prices, including bacon and egg or steak and egg rolls, simple pasta dishes such as ravioli or lasagna, or more substantial plates of fish and chips or pork chops.

Ir-Rizzu

49 Xatt Is-Sajjieda, Marsaxlokk ☎21/651569. Daily 11.30am–2.30pm & 6.30–10.30pm. The largest of Marsaxlokk's clutch of seafront restaurants also has the largest menu and does brisk business in a lobby-like room decorated in white and pale blue. The extensive menu consists mostly of seafood dishes, all prepared in interesting Maltese or Italian ways, although the service is a trifle hectic, and the decor a little impersonal. Mains start from around €7.

▼ LAMPUKI FISH AT MARSAXLOKK MARKET

▲ SEAFOOD AT IR-RIZZU

Kingfisher

Wied Iż-Żurrieq ☎21/647908. June–Sept Tues–Sun 11am–3pm & 7–10pm; Oct–May Tues–Sun 11am–3pm, plus Sat 7–10pm. Arguably the best of the village's half-dozen similar outfits, with no-nonsense portions – albeit overcooked – of Maltese dishes such as spaghetti with octopus, pasta with Maltese sausage and peppered cheese (*ġbejniet*), as well as a full range of Italian pizzas, and fresh fish of the day; prices average €7 per dish, excluding fish.

La Capanna

60 Xatt Is-Sajjieda, Marsaxlokk ☎21/657755. Tues–Sun noon–2.30pm & 6.30–10.30pm. Another small fish restaurant with a mixture of traditional and modern dishes, including pasta with either octopus cooked in white wine and herbs or with squid cooked in its own ink, garlic and oil, as well as grilled fish or a platter of shellfish. Main dishes start at €8.

Pisces

89 Xatt Is-Sajjieda, Marsaxlokk ☎21/654956. Tues–Sun 11am–10.30pm. The most delectable and creative cooking in town, mixing traditional recipes such as fish soup (€4.19) alongside more elaborate concoctions such as roasted grouper crusted with lemon and served with rocket and herb oil (€12.81). However this small place falters on the decor, with an interior full of kitsch trimmings and with garish yellow walls. Fortunately, in good weather you can sit outdoors on the water's edge.

Żejtun Band Club

Misraħ G. Boniċl, Żejtun. Daily 7am–midnight. The town band club has a dull café that serves drinks and grub such as Maltese *ftira* bread with various fillings, including steak and egg, bacon and egg, Maltese sausage, and the traditional filling of tuna, oil and tomato paste. There's also a delicious baked rice with bolognaise sauce and masala spices; prices are all below €2.

Gozo

With a hilly terrain dissected by deep verdant valleys, Gozo has a distinctly different character to Malta. Although massive Baroque churches dominate the townscapes, the island's historical allure is spread throughout its small towns, which are built in concentric circles around central squares. Historical monuments of note only amount to a handful; Gozo's attraction lies in its affable people, early-to-bed lifestyle, rural tranquility and scenic outdoors – particularly the coastline, which is dominated by headlands and large bays in the north, and a girdle of cliffs interspersed with gorges in the south. Unsurprisingly then, Gozo has become a desirable retirement destination for an increasing number of mostly British residents who revel in the slow pace of life. Entertainment mostly revolves around cafés by day and restaurants in the evening, which are scattered throughout the island and mostly serve hearty Gozitan dishes alongside French and Italian classics. Hotels are limited to about a dozen, mostly concentrated in its two seaside towns; most people stay in luxuriously converted farmhouses (or apartments for those on a tighter budget). Gozo remains mostly a family destination, as well as a weekend retreat for wealthy Maltese, but it's also increasingly on the radar of outdoor-sports enthusiasts – the island offers superb scuba diving, rock climbing, canoeing and hiking. The greatest handicap is the inadequate public transport; getting around is slow and frustrating unless you're driving, and buses don't go to some of the most scenic out-of-town spots.

Rabat

Gozo's pleasant capital, Rabat (sometimes called by its English moniker, Victoria), is dominated by the Citadel and defined by its main street, **Triq-Ir Repubblika**, which cuts across the town and has the island's largest concentration of shops. From a visitor's point of view, however, it's the old part of town that invites exploration, its maze of alleys lined with Baroque townhouses with handsome old doors, elaborately carved stone balconies and niches containing Catholic icons. It's a quiet, traffic-free area bounded at the north by **Pjazza Indipendenza**, a pedestrianized square laid out in front of the **Banca Giuratale**, an attractive circular Baroque building from 1733 that is now the town hall. The morning tourist market in the square offers a hotchpotch of kitsch souvenirs, but the cafés surrounding it have outdoor tables from where you can

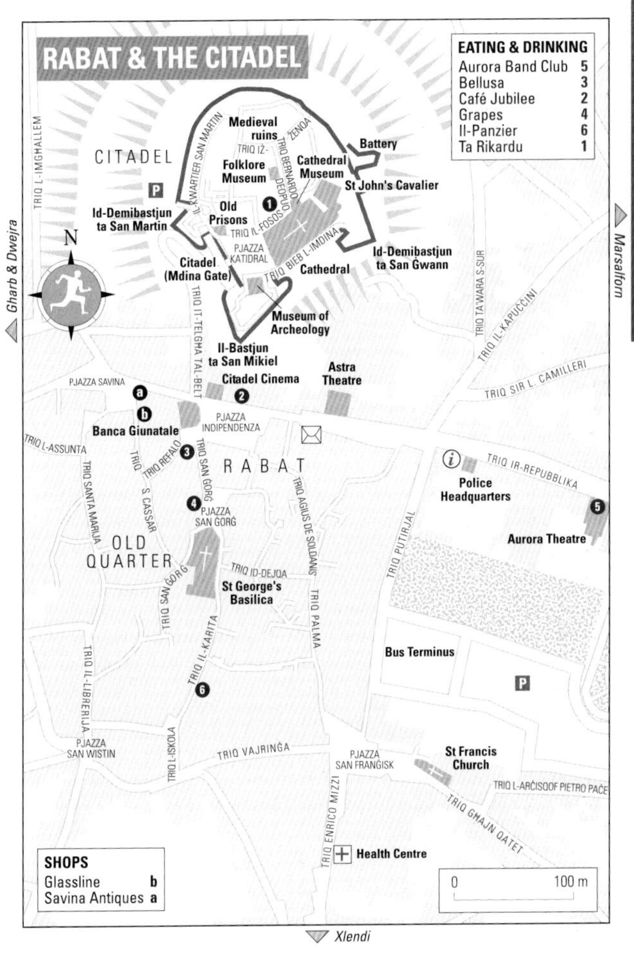

soak up the scene. The square adjoins another to the south, Pjazza San Ġorġ, dominated by the ornate **St George's Basilica** (daily 7am–noon & 2.30–7.30pm; free), the most sumptuously Baroque of Gozo's churches. Built between 1672 and 1778, and tinkered with over the years, the Baroque exterior gives way to an opulent interior covered in marble and featuring a grand canopied altar. St George appears in several notable artworks – look for Mattia Preti's painting on the left-hand side of the nave, Stefano Erardi's altarpiece, and two paintings by Francesco Zahra in the chancel. As you continue past the church, two alleyways wind through the old quarter – wandering towards the southeast eventually brings you into **Pjazza San Franġisk**, Rabat's largest plaza, another

▲ BANCA GIURATALE, RABAT

place where you can relax at a café table under the shade of ficus trees.

The Citadel

Gozo's bulwark castle, commanding a ridge overlooking Rabat, is the island's oldest settlement and prime historical sight. Originally built during Roman rule, it was later destroyed and rebuilt twice. Its walls were last breached in 1551 by the Muslim corsair Dragut Rias, who dragged virtually the entire Gozitan population into slavery – following this it was rebuilt in the seventeenth century. Though less than 200m long by 200m wide, it's a place to linger and take in its wonderful medieval ambience as well as its clutch of museums, and walk around the perimeter fortifications to admire the panoramic views of Gozo's undulating landscape – the Citadel is Gozo's second-highest point.

The first building beyond the Citadel's gates is Gozo's **cathedral** (daily 9.30am–4.30pm; €3), designed by the celebrated Maltese architect Lorenzo Gafa and built between 1697 and 1711. Gafa achieved the difficult task of evoking grandeur in a restricted space by raising the structure on a podium fronted by a wide flight of stairs. However, funds ran out before the dome was built, and the "flat dome" now features the cathedral's most outstanding artwork – a spectacular trompe l'oeil painting of a false dome inside. The **Cathedral Museum** at the back of the church (separate entrance on Triq Il-Fosos; same hours and ticket as cathedral) holds historical riches amassed by the church. The small collection's highlights are the rich tapestries and a fantastic set of paintings called the *Polyptych of Santa Marija*, painted in the sixteenth century.

Visiting Gozo

Ferries between Ċirkewwa in Malta and Mġarr Harbour in Gozo are the main link between the islands. Operating 24 hours, ferries normally run every 45 minutes during much of the day, and every two hours in the evenings and at night; journey time is 25 minutes. Foot-passenger tickets cost €4.66, and it's €15.72 for car and driver; for schedules and more information, call ⓣ21/556016 or visit ⓦwww.gozochannel.com.

Gozo's bus station on Triq Putirjal in Rabat is served by ten routes that make return trips to all of Gozo's towns; in summer, the routes are expanded to cover Dwejra and Ramla Bay. Of the ten services, the #25 to Mġarr Harbour runs every thirty minutes or so; the rest run less frequently, stop between noon and 4pm, and services wind down at around 7pm. You can pick up an up-to-date bus schedule from the tourist office on Triq Ir-Repubblika, Rabat, Gozo (see p.163), or on the transport pages of ⓦwww.gozo.gov.mt; you can also call ⓣ21/562040.

▲ PJAZZA SAN FRANĠISK, RABAT

The other focus points of a wander around the Citadel are its four museums, only three of which are worth checking out (all daily 9am–5pm; €2.30 for individual museum entry, or €4.66 for a combined ticket for all four; Ⓦ www.heritagemalta.org).

Prime among them is the **Archeology Museum**, a small repository of archeological relics discovered in Gozo, spanning all periods from the Neolithic to the Arabic era; top exhibits include the fascinating cluster of Neolithic stone figurines unearthed from an underground burial site in the 1990s, an ancient skeleton interred in an urn in the Phoenician period and, from the Arabic epoch, a tombstone with a long and poetic dedication.

The **Folklore Museum** holds mildly diverting implements of traditional trades, largest of which is the mule-driven wheat mill, but it's the building itself that's more interesting, a medieval Siculo-Norman house that's full of nooks and crannies.

Smaller still, the **Old Prisons** built in the early seventeenth century hold an illuminating exhibition on the Knights' military architecture in Gozo in the former guard room and, in the cells themselves, you can see the graffiti left by former inmates – the most frequent motifs are the outline of a palm (a form of signature) and galleys whose masts each mark a year of sentence served.

The fourth museum, the Natural History Museum, is of marginal interest with its specialized panels that illustrate Gozo's geology, as well as some ad-hoc displays dedicated to flora and fauna, such as worn-out stuffed birds.

▼ RABAT FISH MARKET

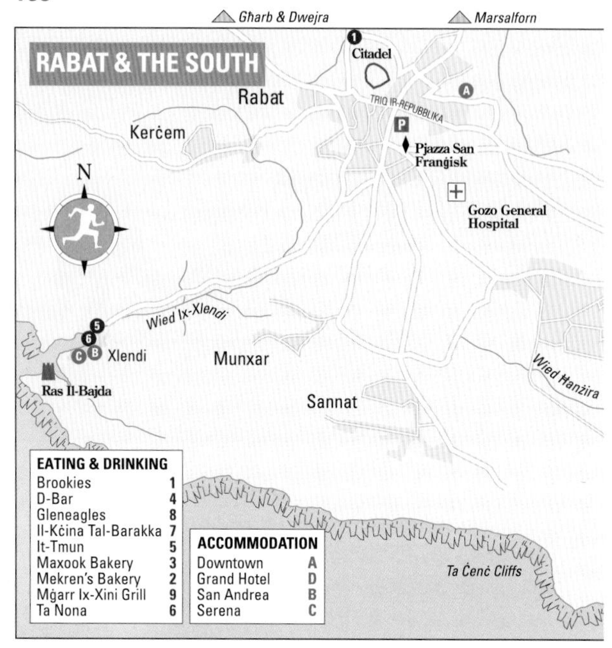

Xewkija

Bus #42 & #43 from Rabat. The main reason to visit Xewkija – a quiet town of empty, shaded streets, with a central old quarter of attractive townhouses with lovely Baroque balconies – is to see the massive **St John the Baptist Church** on Pjazza San Ġwann Battista (daily 6am–noon & 4–7pm; free), whose dome is visible from all over Gozo. The Baroque design – a circular floor plan tapering upwards towards the dome, framed by a bell tower detached from the main structure – is by the Italian Giuseppe Damato. Its dimensions are impressive: supported by eight internal pillars, the dome is the tallest in Malta, while the building's internal volume is only slightly smaller than St Peter's Cathedral in Rome. It's an awe-inspiring structure which prompts contemplation of the faith and dedication that motivated parishioners to endure the hardship of building it; it took

▼ THE CITADEL, RABAT

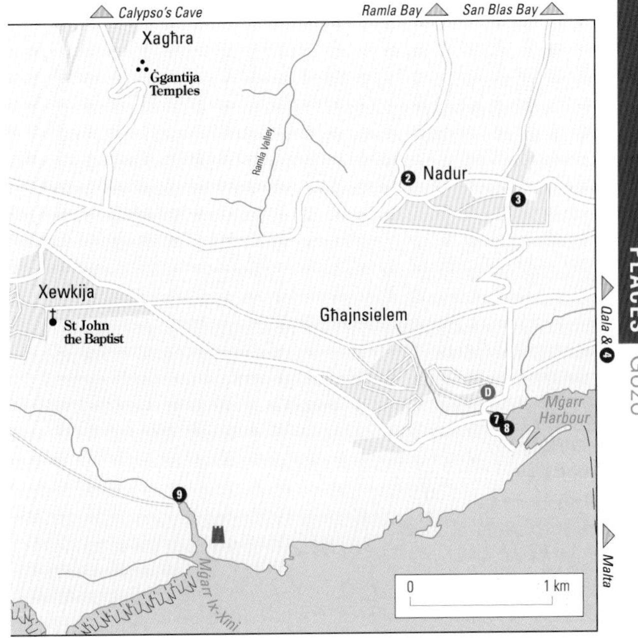

them from 1951 to the early 1990s to complete it, and much of the stone used in the construction was hauled up by hand and in donkey carts.

Wied Ħanżira and Mġarr Ix-Xini

The signposted road from Xewkija to Mġarr Ix-Xini meanders past farms along the south flank of the dramatic **Wied Ħanżira**, a gorge cut into the bedrock by an ancient river – now a popular spot for rock-climbing (see p.170). The valley deepens as it gets closer to the coast, and then meets the sea at **Mġarr Ix-Xini**, a tranquil fjord fronted by a small patch of pebbly shore, where the transparent water beckons you in for a dip. Mġarr Ix-Xini translates as "the harbour of the galleys", harking back to the time when it provided a hidden anchorage for corsairs' frequent raids on Gozo. At the mouth of the bay lie the crumbling remains of a coastal watchtower whose construction by the Knights in 1658 effectively deterred the activities of the marauders. There's no public transport here, but Mġarr Ix-Xini is a pleasant half-hour walk from Xewkija. The country road peters out at the bottom of the fjord, where there's a tiny car park and a rustic restaurant that cooks up fresh seafood in summer (see p.154).

Ta Ċenċ Cliffs

Bus #50 & #51 from Rabat. Just outside the nondescript town of Sannat, the land falls sharply into the sea at well-signposted Ta Ċenċ, a dramatic and dizzying 150-metre drop. With sweeping views of the sea stretching towards the horizon, it's a very scenic spot for a walk, and the rocky garigue (a rugged habitat of hardy bushes) supports some interesting local fauna and flora. Clumps of rock centuary – Malta's national plant, with small, succulent leaves and fluffy mauve flowers in summer – cling to the cliff edge, and the area is a favoured haunt of the blue rock thrush, the national bird, easily identifiable by its melodious warble, dark brown or blue plumage, and habit of flicking its tailfeathers up and down. Ta Ċenċ is best known, however, for the 1000 pairs of Cory's shearwaters that nest in crags on the cliff face, one of the largest colonies in the Mediterranean. They spend all day at sea, so you can only observe them if you visit on moonless nights during the May to August nesting season when – although you're unlikely to catch a glimpse of their dark, smoky plumage – their raucous and melancholy meows rise to a din that sounds eerily human.

Xlendi

Bus #87 from Rabat. At the mouth of the Xlendi Valley, which winds down scenically from the outskirts of Rabat, Xlendi is Gozo's second largest seaside resort. The town is dominated by a thick fabric of apartment blocks climbing up to one side of the cliff-lined Xlendi Bay, a claustrophobic, dense development that belies the bay's character – a sheltered gorge with gently lapping waters and a tranquil waterfront lined with cafés and restaurants. Yet openness and spectacular scenery is only a short stroll away via an old path that connects to the promenade along the southeastern flank of the bay; the path, built by the Knights, leads to the coastal tower at the hunchback promontory called Ras Il-Bajda at the mouth of the bay. The land here peters out at a globigerina-limestone plateau, sculpted into waves by wind erosion, which tilts down to the waterline and offers sweeping views of the sheer cliffs of the southern coast. The cliff face across the bay was until a few generations ago a favoured spot for the area's so-called "climbing fishermen", who inched down the cliff to ledges near the bottom to fish in

▼ MĠARR IX-XINI

▲ XLENDI BRIDGE AND BAY

the deep waters. It's also home to nesting Cory's shearwaters in spring and summer, and at night you can hear their doleful mewling. From Ras Il-Bajda the deep-blue water out in the bay beckons – you can dive in from rocky outcrops, or walk in and out at a spot where the rocks step into the water; the rock face that slopes sharply underwater also offers excellent snorkelling (sea urchins, octopus and starfish are common). Another way to get closer to the sweep of cliffs across the bay, and to explore the caves gouged at sea level, is in a canoe or paddle boat available for rent (€5) in the summer months at the promenade in the inner mouth of Xlendi Bay.

Marsalforn

Bus #21 from Rabat. On the opposite northern coast from Xlendi, Marsalforn is Gozo's largest seaside resort, consisting of a ribbon of apartment blocks spread along the coast of the large, airy bay. Despite the dense buildings, the bay has an open feel and for much of the year it feels like a resort in low season – only on summer evenings does a genteel bustle of strollers pick up and the seafront restaurants fill up. There's some traditional colour at Il-Menqa, a small breakwater-enclosed harbour on the east flank of Marsalforn Bay that's the docking station for a dwindling number of brightly painted *luzzi* fishing boats; otherwise, there isn't much else to distract you from lounging at a café. You can swim at a small sandy beach at the inner mouth of the bay, but it's rather exposed to passers-by and the sea bed is rocky, so most locals prefer to swim off the rocks that trace the waterline along the west side of the bay, where the promenade gives way to the rocky shoreline (there are ladders for getting in and out). There's better swimming five minutes' walk east of town at Għar Qawqla, where you can jump in from a limestone plateau; stairs also lead to the water, and there are sun-loungers for rent.

Xwejni saltpans

1km west of Marsalforn, no public transport. Hundreds of depressions gouged into the soft yellow globigerina limestone, Gozo's saltpans form an intricate web of abstract patterns, and take up a fairly sizeable stretch of scenic coastline, some 2km long by 50m wide. During winter, heavy waves splatter seawater over the rocks to fill the pans; this evaporates during

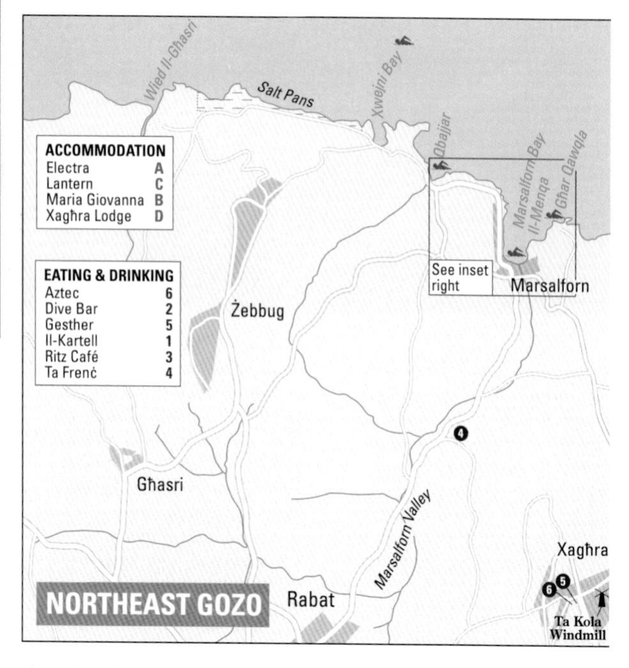

the calm of the summer, leaving crusts of crystal salt. If you visit in August, you'll see gangs of workers shovelling the salt into bags; the uncrushed crystals are sold in most local supermarkets. Despite the commercial slant, the pans are beautiful, particularly during winter, when the reflection of the sky in the pan-water makes it look like a field of mirrors.

Wied Il-Għasri

No public transport. A deep, snaking gorge some 300m long with a creek at the bottom, Wied Il-Għasri is reachable via the right fork of the road beyond the last salt pans and almost directly north of the Ġordan Lighthouse (see p.147). The only human intervention here is the flight of stairs pickaxed into the side of the cliff to provide access to the inner mouth of the creek, where a tiny pebbly shore gives way to the narrow body of water whose colour ranges from green to deep blue. This is an excellent spot for snorkelling; look out for rays, deep-water fish and some curious underwater topography towards the outer reaches of the creek.

Xagħra

Buses #64 and #65 from Rabat.
One of Gozo's largest towns, Xagħra sprawls over a series of ridges and bluffs – at one end it's up the slope from Marsalforn and at another end it looms over Rabat. It's a comparatively busy place, with an attractive and lively town square, Pjazza Vittorja, fringed by oleander trees and handsome Baroque townhouses with old colonial-era bars sitting alongside modern restaurants.

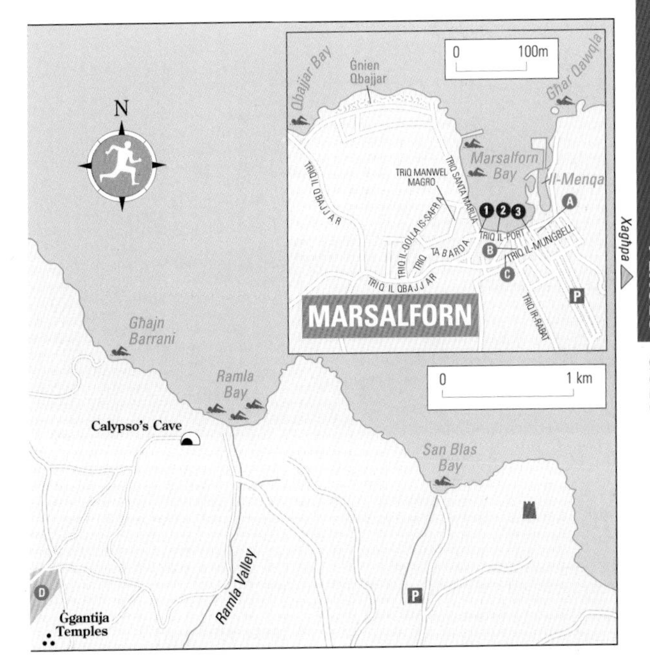

At the head of the square is the parish church, with its ornate bell towers and dome; it was designed by Maltese priest Karlu Żimech, and built in the mid-eighteenth century. Its marble-panelled interior (daily 6–10am & 5–7pm; free) holds some good paintings and an exquisite organ.

Ġgantija temples

Triq L-Imqades, Xagħra ⓣ21/553194, ⓦwww.heritagemalta.org. Daily 9am–5pm. €3.50. Buses #64 & #65 from Rabat. Of all the Neolithic temples in the Maltese islands, the two at Ġgantija are perhaps the most evocative and impressive; they're also the oldest freestanding man-made structures in the world, erected in around 3600 BC. The complex lay under an accumulation of rubble for thousands of years before being discovered and excavated in 1827. Since then erosion has taken a heavy toll (some sections teeter dangerously close to collapse), but the half-ruined

▼ GHAR QAWQLA, NEAR MARSALFORN

▲ PJAZZA VITTORJA, XAĠHRA

edifice remains an imposing sight with its megalithic walls projecting over the bluff it's situated on – the largest megalith, estimated to weigh 55 tonnes, is as large as a pickup truck. The circular complex itself is comprised of the North and South Temples that share one perimeter wall. The first, the five-apsed **North Temple**, holds some crumbling remains of simple altars – flat slabs of rock resting on two upright stones – but the adjoining **South Temple** is markedly larger, its arrangement more sophisticated and its five apses more protracted. Features of note include a series of bowls cut into the rocks immediately behind the entrance, suggestive of some sort of purification ritual before entry into the temple, while the first apse on the right holds various pieces of stone, carved with eroding spiral motifs, which are arranged in a spatial configuration that obviously had some divine or ceremonial significance. Also lining the passageways are libation holes that are thought to have been used to drain blood from sacrificed animals, and in the second chamber the three altars in the apse to the left survive virtually intact.

Ta Kola Windmill

Triq Il-Mithna, Xaġhra ⓣ21/561071, ⓦwww.heritagemalta.org. Daily 9am–5pm. €2.30. Buses #64 & #65 from Rabat. Now open as a tourist attraction, having ceased commercial wheat-grinding at the beginning of the twentieth century, this attractive two-storey windmill topped by its circular sail-tower was built in 1725. It's worth a visit to see the still- intact original apparatus that turned the grinding stones, a complex series of huge cogwheels fashioned entirely out of timber. Upstairs, you can peruse the re-created millers' living quarters: stark dining and living rooms, two bedrooms and a kitchen decked out with a traditional *kenur*, a stone hearth used for stewing.

Calypso's Cave

Buses #64 & #65 from Rabat. Perched on a bluff above the sea, Calypso's Cave is misleadingly touted as the legendary grotto inhabited by the nymph Calypso on an island called Ogygia in Homer's *Odyssey*, where she kept Odysseus captive through love for seven years. Although there is some evidence that Gozo was once called Ogygia, the proof that this is the true Calypso's Cave is circumstantial (muddling things further, some researchers also claim that the real cave is situated in a valley in Mellieħa). Indeed, it's unclear how Gozo's cavern requisitioned the title – perhaps because of the marvellous view here, which is the main reason to visit. It's a gorgeous scene of clay slopes tumbling down to the orange sand of Ramla Bay, and rolling inland into Ramla Valley – you can pick out the town of Nadur on a ledge at the valley's far side. The miserably unimpressive cave itself, formed by fissures in the rock surface, is not worth the effort of climbing into.

Ramla Bay

Bus #42 from Rabat July–Sept only.

Enclosed by twin headlands, Ramla Bay is among the most stunning beaches in the Mediterranean. It's set at the mouth of a large valley; the bay is flanked by high ridges, and the beach itself – a strip of unusual, bright orange-coloured sand – gives way to a sweep of clear shallow sea. At the back of the beach the sand rises into dunes that are bound by tamarisk trees, the only sand-dune habitat in the Maltese islands, and home to rare plants and insects – avoid lying on the sand dunes, let alone camping or having a barbecue. The bay also holds two historical attractions: an underground wall built by the Knights to hinder enemy boats from landing, and, on the eastern flank of the bay, a *fougasse* – a rock-cut mortar that was designed to be filled with rocks and gunpowder and fired on enemy vessels attempting to break through the underwater wall.

Ramla is attractive at any time of the year – it's a great spot for a stroll in winter, and the best beach in the islands for swimming in the summer – but it gets understandably crowded in summer. For a quieter spot, there is a small sandy creek on the western flank of the bay, reachable via a ten-minute walk from the beach proper along a path that skirts the shoreline.

Parking for Ramla Bay is on the wide access road and private fields that are turned into a temporary car park in the summer; just before the beach, a couple of operators rent umbrellas and sun loungers, and kiosks serve drinks and snacks.

San Blas Bay

Buses #42 & #43 from Rabat to Nadur.

A small, sandy beach with lurid orange sand, San Blas is like a miniature version of Ramla

▼ TA KOLA WINDMILL

– cut into bluffs of rocky cliffs and set at the bottom of a verdant valley known for its citrus groves. San Blas has been left in its pristine natural state – the only commercial activity is a portable kiosk where you can rent umbrellas, sun loungers and canoes, as well as have drinks and dig into an excellent hotdog, and it's a scenic spot for a day by the sea, splashing in its shallow water or sunbathing. Another possibility is to rent a canoe (€5) and go exploring the dramatic landscape of meandering cliff-crowned headlands which peter out at the waterline in jumbles of massive boulders on either side of the bay.

The downside of San Blas's natural glory is limited access: unless you're driving, you have to walk from Nadur's town centre (a thirty-minute walk), and even if you're driving, the farmers' access road (which starts when the last houses peter out on the ridge) is a narrow concrete strip that is only drivable half-way down, and fills up with cars very quickly on summer afternoons (you might have to park at the clearing near the last houses, and walk the 2km to the beach).

Ta' Pinu Basilica

☎21/556187. Daily 7am–12.15pm & 1.30–7pm. Free. Bus #91 from Rabat. A couple of kilometres west of Rabat, the imposing Ta' Pinu Basilica is Malta's primary pilgrimage site. The church had its beginnings as a medieval chapel, but by 1575 had fallen into disrepair and was marked for demolition. However, the worker who struck the first sledgehammer blow apparently broke his arm – an incident interpreted as a divine sign, which led to the chapel being spared. In 1883, Ta' Pinu gained more notoriety when a local fieldworker, Karmela Grima, heard a disembodied voice summoning her to the chapel, where it instructed her to "recite three Hail Marys in honour of the three days my body was confined to the tomb". Grima's story spread like wildfire, and islanders started making pilgrimages to the chapel. The present church was built between 1920 and 1932 to accommodate the ever-increasing number of pilgrims, who still visit today.

▼ TA' PINU BASILICA

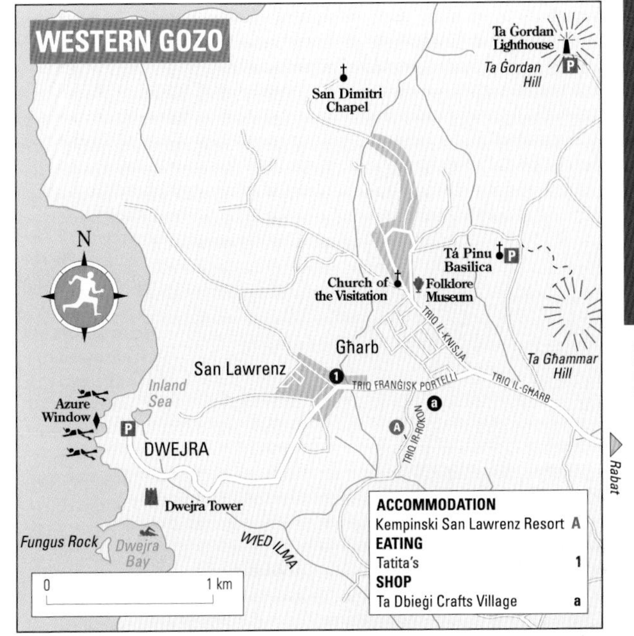

The rich Romanesque exterior is complemented by its large size and setting, in the midst of open countryside, and its interior is packed with ornate stone sculptures. But most interesting is the original medieval chapel itself at the back of the present church, reached through corridors on either side of the altar that are cluttered with votive offerings left by those allegedly healed by the Madonna's miracles. The compact chapel has whitewashed walls and a simple but moving altarpiece painted by the Italian artist Amadeo Perugino depicting eight angels crowning the Madonna in heaven (the crown, attached to the painting, is made of gold). Opposite the church, the stations of the Cross have been reproduced in life-size marble statues lining a route up the Ta Għammar hill. The view from the top of the hill, which takes in northwest Gozo's motley sweep of fields and compact towns, is worth the walk.

Ġordan Hill

Bus #91 from Rabat. A couple of kilometres north of Ta' Pinu – and visible from Ta' Pinu – the road leads through the edge of the town of Għasri to the table-top summit of Ġordan Hill, girdled by an amber, jagged cliff face and slopes of blue clay, and topped by a lighthouse that now serves as a meteorological station. The panoramic views of the northwest's undulating landscape from the top of the hill are excellent, and well worth the journey up; you can also take a short walk along a path that loops around the hilltop.

There's a small car park on the shoulder of the hill just below the cliff.

Għarb

Bus #1, #2 and #91 from Rabat. Għarb is the most traditional and the sleepiest town in the Maltese islands, and has seen relatively little new development – though it has become something of a favourite place to own a second home, with many of its buildings now converted into suitably plush pads. The swimming pools and landscaped gardens haven't detracted from Għarb's rustic appeal, though, and it's a pleasant place to explore, with plenty of ornate townhouses fanning out from its attractive central square. The **Church of the Visitation** (open daily for services only 6–8.30am & 5–7pm), completed in 1732, boasts an unusual and striking concave facade. The ornate low dome is framed by two bell towers, and the striking female statues on the facade represent Faith (standing above the door), Hope (to the left) and Charity (to the right).

▼ GHARB TOWN SQUARE

Opposite the church, a restored eighteenth-century townhouse holds the **Folklore Museum** (Ⓣ21/561929; Mon–Sat 9.30am–4pm, Sun 9.30am–noon; €3.50), whose collection, spread over 28 rooms, provides some interesting insight into traditional life in Gozo. It centres on the tools, machinery and manufacturing techniques of small-scale local industries that operated in Gozo before the advent of electricity and motor machinery in the early twentieth century, some of which are still in use today. Each room is dedicated to a different trade, and captions describe the exhibits and explain how they were employed.

Dwejra

Bus #91 from Rabat, Mon–Sat only. An undulating landscape shaped by geological rifts and characterized by bowl-shaped valleys, its coastline pockmarked with bays, Dwejra's distorted, crater-like topography has a bleak, alien attraction, and makes for some very scenic walking. Offshore, the underwater cliffs, valleys, ledges, massive plateaux and deep caves supporting soft coral offer excellent scuba diving (see p.168). The bus from Rabat drops you off at a car park near the **Azure Window**, a picturesque natural window in the cliffs of almost 100m in height and width that has been created by wave erosion. A minute's walk from here, along a side road that strikes off from the main access road, is the **Inland Sea**, a landlocked body of seawater connected to the Mediterranean via a tunnel in the towering cliff face. In the opposite direction, southeast

▲ FOLKLORE MUSEUM, GHARB

of the car park, another path takes you to **Dwejra Tower** (Mon–Fri 8am–3pm; free), one of the coastal defence chain built by the Knights; although the tower's interior is small and unremarkable, the views from the roof are excellent.

Beyond the tower is the horseshoe-shaped **Dwejra Bay**, whose shallow water is almost pitch black due to a thick blanket of seaweed that gets washed in by the northwesterly waves. At the mouth of the bay, **Fungus Rock** (Il-Ġebla Tal-General) soars 70m out of the sea into a stout pinnacle. The rock became renowned in the eighteenth century following the discovery of a parasitic plant growing here, which was thought to have wide-ranging medicinal and mythological powers. By 1746, the Knights had put the rock under 24-hour guard to preserve the plant for the privileged use of European royals and rulers (they believed that it grew only on this rock). Scientific analysis eventually discounted the alleged medicinal properties. However, the rock remains out of bounds today to protect the plant, called Malta Fungus, one of the world's rarest species – phallus-shaped and covered in velvety brownish-red flowers, it grows abundantly here, but is extremely rare elsewhere in the Mediterranean.

Hotels

Downtown

Triq L-Ewropa, Rabat ⓣ22/108000, ⓦwww.downtown.com.mt. The most strategic place to stay on the island if you lack private transport – in summer guests can take the free transport to a different beach each day. The spacious en-suite rooms have hardwood furniture and warm colours and come with fridges, a/c, phones, TVs, large beds and a writing or dressing table. Doubles €60, breakfast included.

Grand Hotel

Mġarr ⓣ21/563840, ⓦwww.grandhotelmalta.com. Imposing hybrid of Baroque and Neoclassical design overlooking Mġarr harbour. The pleasant, standard en-suite rooms have a/c, phones and TVs; those with sea views are more expensive.

▲ INLAND SEA, DWEJRA

Doubles from €70, breakfast included.

Kempinski San Lawrenz Resort

Triq Ir-Rokon, San Lawrenz ⓣ22/110000, ⓦwww.kempinski-gozo.com. Gozo's most upscale hotel is a Baroque-style building with coffered ceilings, loggia-framed balconies and plenty of paintings, and is surrounded by hills and agricultural land. The facilities are extensive, including a hammam and a spa, and the pastel-coloured rooms are airy and comfortable. Doubles from €230, including breakfast.

San Andrea

St Simon Street, Xlendi ⓣ21/565555, ⓦwww.hotelsanandrea.com. Twenty-eight small yet tastefully decorated en-suite rooms with warm colours; the rooms have a/c, balconies, phones and TVs. Doubles €60, breakfast included.

Serena

St Simon Street, Xlendi ⓣ21/553719, ⓦwww.serena.com.mt. Designed in pompous, almost garish, Baroque, this new building offers good-value, largish a/c studios with double beds, a mini-kitchen, TVs, phones and large bathrooms, and with good views of Xlendi from the balconies. Doubles €100, breakfast included.

Guesthouses

Electra

Triq Il-Wied, Marsalforn ⓣ21/556196. Marsalforn's budget option, this basic family-run property has fifteen plain doubles with en-suite bathrooms, and some single rooms with shared bathrooms, and balconies that overlook the bay. Doubles €35 and singles €18, breakfast included.

Lantern

Triq Il-Munġbell, Marsalforn ⓣ21/562365, ⓕ21/556285. The newly refurbished twelve en-suite rooms (including some triples) are bright but a bit stuffy; furniture is plain and the rooms come with a small bathroom, TV and fridge (and optional a/c for an extra €10 daily). Doubles €50, breakfast included.

Maria Giovanna

41 Triq Ir-Rabat, Marsalforn ⓣ21/553630, ⓦwww.tamariagozo.com. The fifteen en-suite rooms are nicely decorated with old-style furniture, and equipped with a/c and wireless Internet. The price is attractive for this standard of accommodation – book in advance in the high season. Doubles €50, breakfast included.

Bed and breakfast

Xagħra Lodge

Triq Dun Ġorġ Preca, Xagħra ⓣ21/562362, ⓔxaghralodge@waldonet.net.mt. Run by British expats and discreetly located in residential Xagħra, the house is decorated with mahogany furniture, chandeliers and elaborate curtains. The en-suite, a/c rooms include family and honeymoon rooms. Common facilities include a small pool and a standard Chinese restaurant. Doubles €60, breakfast included.

Shops

Glassline

Pjazza Savina, Rabat ⓣ79888444. Daily 10am–5pm. Sells a range of creative work using glass – including necklaces and earrings, stained glass (made with painted glass and lead pigments), and decorative pieces such as bowls. Prices vary, starting from €10 for simple earrings, and rising to €40 for a necklace made of streaks of molten silver embedded in the glass. Stained glass starts from €40.

Savina Antiques

Pjazza Savina, Rabat. Daily 9am–3pm. A large assortment of relatively inexpensive antique bric-a-brac arrayed on the pavement, mostly traditional Maltese brassware.

Ta Dbieġi Crafts Village

Triq Franġisk Portelli, San Lawrenz. Daily: June–Sept 9.30am–6pm; Oct–May 9.30am–4pm. A cluster of artisan workshops producing and selling good-quality local crafts such as candles, pottery, lace, brassware, colourful blown glass and a particularly creative range of ceramics, including custom-made pieces.

Cafés and bars

Aurora Band Club

Triq Ir-Repubblika, Rabat. Daily 8am–11pm. Large café that serves inexpensive coffees and drinks, and fast food such as burgers and *pastizzi*, as well as English breakfasts and steaks. There are also snooker tables and Internet access.

Bellusa

34 Pjazza Indipendenza, Rabat ⓣ21/556243. Daily: May–Oct 7am–9pm, Nov–April until 6pm. Good coffee, as well as

▼ BELLUSA

Clubs in Gozo

Gozo's clubbing revolves around four venues that open in different seasons. On Fridays between June and October, the only club is the *Rook* in Qbajjar, the seaside town east of Marsalforn (free), a Knights-era fort converted into an open-air disco, while Saturday nights see the crowds head to *La Grotta* on Xlendi Road, Xlendi (€5), another venue from the same owners. Both start at 10pm, but fill up at around 1am and then wind down by dawn; in both the music is mostly a mixture of pop and beats, all poorly mixed. *La Grotta* is redeemed to some extent by a second dance-floor that is dedicated to more modern techno, but still nothing special. Between November and May, these venues go into hibernation, and two clubs in Rabat are resuscitated for Saturday nights only. These are *Ku*, near the Citadel off Marsalforn Road (€5), with a retro Eighties-style decor and poorly mixed hybrid of pop and dance, and *XS* (part of the *Aurora Band Complex*; entrance from near the car park; €5). The latter is Gozo's best club with a good sound system, a minimalist design and better dance music than its competitor. It also has the largest number of one-off events with good international DJs; similar events are also held at *Ku* and *La Grotta*.

pastizzi, pizza and other meals and snacks, served outdoors in the atmospheric Pjazza Indipendenza by the attentive and chatty proprietors.

Café Jubilee

Pjazza Indipendenza, Rabat ☎21/558921. Daily 8am–1am. A café-bar that attracts regulars for its coffee and daytime snacks, and becomes more of a quiet bar with good music in the evenings, particularly during winter when it's busiest.

Dive Bar

Triq Il-Port, Marsalforn. June–Sept daily 6pm–4am; Oct–May Fri & Sat 6pm–3am. A friendly bar whose interior mimics that of a submarine, and tends to attract a late-night crowd; music ranges from pop to techno.

Gleneagles

10 Victory St, Mġarr Harbour ☎27556543. Daily 2pm–1am. Opened in 1885, this former fishermen's watering hole, decorated with nautical curios, caters for a wider clientele as well as fishermen. The tables set on the balcony afford good views of the quaint and colourful harbour.

Grapes

Pjazza San Ġorġ, Rabat ☎79473536. Daily 8am–3am. A friendly wine-bar and café serving a range of drinks and platters of traditional antipasti, as well as traditionally cooked rabbit, all served outdoors in the atmospheric square. It becomes a fully fledged bar in the evenings, and it gets particularly busy on winter weekends.

Ritz Café

Triq Il-Wied, Marsalforn. Daily noon–4am. Long-established place with indoor and outdoor seating on the waterfront, serving coffees and snacks including pizzas (€5). It becomes more of a bar in the evenings, when the regulars play table games or watch TV.

Ta Nona

Xatt Ix-Xlendi, Xlendi ☎21/550869. Daily: June–Sept 10am–4am; Oct–May 10am–4pm & 8–11pm. This small bar, with curio prints cluttering its stone walls, and tables on the promenade, makes a sunny spot for afternoon teas and coffees and a bit of people-watching. They also serve palatable one-plate meals including omelettes, steaks, and pizzas for modest prices.

Restaurants

Aztec

Pjazza Vittorja, Xagħra ☎21/564942. Mon & Wed–Sun 6–10.30pm. The best restaurant in the square, it serves some traditional dishes – such as Gozo-style ravioli – alongside an eclectic daily roster of specials such as deer in tomato sauce infused with oregano and other herbs. About €15 for mains.

Brookies

1/2 Triq Wied Sara, Rabat ☎21/559524. Mon & Wed–Sun 6.30–10.30pm. Set in an old restored townhouse decorated with abstract art, the French cuisine here is influenced by Gozitan cooking and ingredients. The menu, which changes seasonally, might include risotto with zucchini (€7) or pork fillet cooked in figs and port wine (€12).

D-Bar

Pjazza San Ġużepp, Qala ☎21/556242. Daily 6.30–10.30pm, Sat & Sun also noon–2pm. Tucked away in the town square of Qala, Gozo's easternmost town, this place serves Gozo's best pizzas, made from dense traditional dough and including the traditional anchovy pizza alongside those with more unusual toppings such as mussels, crab-meat, prawns and two cheeses (€8) or rocket leaves, mozzarella and Parma ham (€7.50).

Gesther

Triq Tmienja Ta' Settembru, Xagħra ☎21/556621. Mon–Sat noon–2.30pm. Small, unassuming restaurant that excels in Gozitan home-cooking. The simply prepared dishes – marrow soup, roast lamb, stuffed chicken breast and broad bean and goat's cheese pie – are wholesome and tasty. By far the best food in Malta in this price range (around €7 for mains).

▼ MARSALFORN RESTAURANTS

Il-Kartell

Triq Marina, Marsalforn ☎21/556918. June–Sept daily noon–3.30pm & 6–10.30pm; Oct–May Mon, Tues & Thurs–Sun noon–3.30pm & 6–10.30pm. Call ahead to check winter opening hours. Marsalforn's best restaurant, with tables at the water's edge and a menu of traditional Gozitan dishes – the stuffed marrow is particularly good, as is penne with local sausage, sun-dried tomatoes and garlic. About €13 for main courses.

Il-Kċina Tal-Barakka

Triq Manoel de Vilhena, Mġarr Harbour ☎21/556503. May–Oct Tues–Sun 7–10pm. Another place focused on delicious and simply cooked fresh seafood (around €14 for main courses) served up in a cosy little room where the closely packed tables don't leave much elbow room.

Il-Panzier

Triq Il-Karita, Rabat ☎21/559979. Daily noon–2.30pm & 6.30–9.30pm; closed for one month in Dec/Jan. Malta's best Sicilian food, served in a covered courtyard in Rabat's old town, features solid Sicilian specialities, including sea bass baked in oregano and rosemary (€15) or the all-time popular asparagus and cheese bake served with asparagus and tomato sauce (€15).

It-Tmun

3 Triq Mount Carmel, Xlendi ☎21/551571. March–Oct Mon & Wed–Sun noon–2pm & 6.30–10pm; Nov–Feb Fri–Sun noon–2pm & 6.30–10pm but sometimes closed, so call in advance. One of Gozo's best fusion restaurants features a constantly changing menu and an impressive wine list. Traditional seafood platters sit alongside more adventurous dishes such as a thick soup of tomatoes, onions, prawns, mussels, and other seafood, and a grilled quail in coconut Thai curry. Main courses for about €14.

Mġarr Ix-Xini Grill

Mġarr Ix-Xini ☎79854007. Daily: 11am–4pm, June–Sept also 6–9pm. A simple formula – fresh

▼ TATITA'S

Gozitan ftiras

Delectable traditional Gozitan pizzas – called *ftiras* – are still made by two bakeries in Nadur town. Traditionally, *ftiras* came in two forms – either topped with anchovies, tomatoes, onions and potatoes, or as closed pizzas stuffed with sheep's cheese beaten in eggs – but now the bakeries have introduced other varieties. Best of the two bakeries is Maxook Bakery (21 Triq San Ġakbu, Nadur, ☎21/550014; Mon–Sat 8am–8pm, Sun noon–8pm), where the dough is still made the traditional way from bread dough, and the *ftiras* are cooked in a wood-fired oven; toppings range from the traditional varieties to ones such as local sausage, sliced potatoes and hard-boiled eggs (€4–5). If you prefer a dough that's easier on your teeth, go to Mekren's Bakery (Triq Ħanaq, Nadur, ☎21/552342; daily 9.30am–7pm), which does larger *ftiras* with a crumblier dough but with less choice of toppings (either traditional toppings, or Capricciosa-style; €3–3.50). At both places you need to call and order in advance – by 4pm at Maxook's and by noon at Mekren's – then you can pick up your order any time within opening hours.

seafood either grilled or cooked in white wine, garlic, herbs and olive oil, and served with chips and salad – nonetheless makes this place a winner for the tasty plain seafood and setting, with tables set on the shoreline. Around €14 for main courses.

Ta Frenċ

Marsalforn Road, Rabat ☎21/553888. April–Dec daily noon–1.30pm & 7–10pm; Jan–March Fri & Sat noon–1.30pm & 7–10pm, Sun noon–2pm. One of Malta's best restaurants is all-out impressive, set in a converted farmhouse, with an extensive wine list, excellent service and serving creative and rich French cuisine. The menu includes quails stuffed with herbs and cooked with mushrooms, Gozo cheese, honey and red wine (€14.50), or, at the upper end of the scale, lobster cooked with cognac and cream, and served with spinach and tarragon sauce (€38).

Ta Rikardu

4 Triq Il-Fosos, Rabat ☎21/555953. Daily 10am–6pm. Rustic antipasti platters of Maltese sausage, *ġbejniet* sheep's cheese, sun-dried tomatoes, olives, capers, tomatoes and onions cost €7 for two, and there's good home-made wine at €7 per bottle.

Tatita's

Pjazza San Lawrenz, San Lawrenz ☎21/566482. March–Oct daily noon–3pm & 6–10.30pm. Set in an atmospheric townhouse in San Lawrenz's square, the combination of an extensive wine list, good service and a good range of dishes have raised the profile of this place. You can opt for something classic such as *bragioli* (stuffed beef wraps) or rabbit, or go for something more unusual such as calamari stuffed with prawns, peas, rice, clams, marjoram and basil. Main courses around €13.

Comino

Though it looks little more than a barren, sun-baked rock from the sea, tiny Comino (just 2km long by 1.7km wide) harbours a surprising variety of flora and fauna. It also offers breathtaking clifftop scenery, two of the Maltese islands' most alluring beaches and great snorkelling and diving. Throughout the summer, Comino sees its fair share of visitors and the beaches get pretty busy, but for the rest of the year, things are dead quiet. The ideal time to visit is in the spring, when the rocky habitat blooms into a mosaic of flowers, but whatever the time of year, Comino is best seen via a gentle stroll along its single dirt road – it takes just two hours to walk around the entire island.

The Blue Lagoon

The Blue Lagoon is a fitting name for this sweep of turquoise water sandwiched between Comino and its sister islet of Kemmunett. The water is so clear that it's like being in a pool, and you can enjoy the dramatic vista of the cliffs and Comino's tower as you swim between the islands. The downside is that the Blue Lagoon gets hideously overcrowded in summer, when boats packed with day-tripping bathers anchor in the bay from mid-morning until late afternoon. The small patch of sand fronting the lagoon at both ends is tiny and fills up quickly, and even on sunny winter afternoons some touring boats call at the lagoon. If you're looking for privacy and quiet it's best to visit in the morning.

St Mary's Tower

The sheer cliffs and variegated colours of the deep waters beyond the Blue Lagoon serve as a beautiful backdrop to St Mary's Tower, which is perched on the edge of the cliffs. The largest of the Knights' coastal towers – its

▼ VIEW OF COMINO

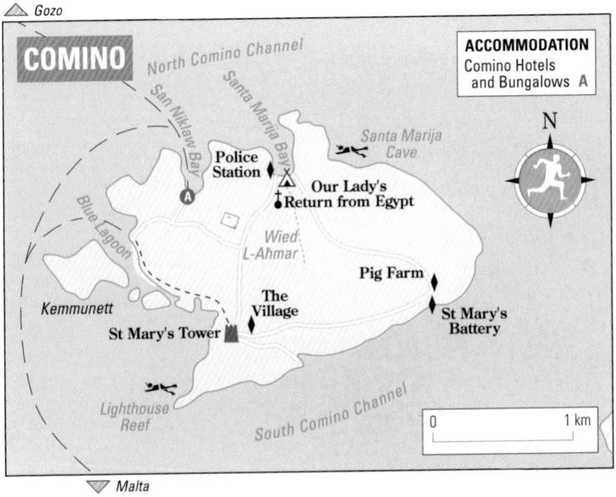

walls are over 5m thick – it was built in 1618 by Grand Master Alof de Wignacourt to serve as a base for the garrison of troops stationed on Comino to protect the island from invasion and to guard the Malta–Gozo channel, a role it continued to serve until the 1990s. It's now in the care of a historical charity that's currently restoring the building and plans to open it regularly as a museum. At the time of writing it was already opening occasionally (the telltale sign when it's open is a raised flag), but even if it's closed, it's worth walking to the cliff edge in front of the tower which affords a peaceful and isolated view over the water. Crevices in the cliffs hereabouts are home to the blue rock thrush, Malta's national bird; you might see the dark blue males or brownish-grey females perched on outcrops performing their characteristic tail-flicks.

Visiting Comino

Only Midas Shuttle offer all-year services (☎99474142), with daily boats between Ċirkewwa and the Blue Lagoon shuttling back and forth on the hour from 9am to 5pm, and costing €9.32 return; services are suspended in bad weather, and are liable to be reduced in winter when demand is low, so it's best to call in advance during low season.

Between April and October Anselma (☎99459389) runs trips from Quay 3 at Gozo's Mġarr Harbour to the Blue Lagoon (or to other landings at San Niklaw Bay or Santa Marija Bay – depending on weather and passengers' demands) for €7; there are return trips on the hour between 10am and 4.20am (and an additional trip at 6pm at the height of the summer).

Also from April to October, the *Comino Hotel*'s boat shuttles guests between Ċirkewwa in Malta, and Mġarr Harbour in Gozo to the landing in San Niklaw Bay, and will take non-guests for €8. It makes a couple of round-trips daily between sunrise and sunset – timings change every year, so call ☎21/529821 for the latest schedule.

▲ ST MARY'S BATTERY

The Village

A horseshoe-shaped two-storey building, with loggias overlooking a courtyard and limestone walls that are slowly being eroded by the sea-spray, the Village was built in 1912. It served as an isolation hospital for plague and cholera victims before becoming the living quarters of a community of 65 people who grew export crops on Comino until the venture hit hard times in the early 1960s. The island's four current inhabitants are the only ones who remained behind, and they now occupy a small part of the building.

St Mary's Battery and Wied L-Aħmar

Continuing east along the coastal road brings you to a shabby and abandoned former pig farm, established here to raise disease-free animals after foot-and-mouth disease decimated Malta's pig stocks in the 1980s. Behind this, at the edge of the cliffs, is **St Mary's Battery**. Built in 1714, it's the best-preserved of the dozens of batteries erected by the Knights in their drive to reinforce Malta's coastal defences. Like its counterparts, it's a semicircular gun platform overlooking the sea, and in its heyday eight cannons poked out of its battlements. Though the battery is currently closed to the public, you can still see into its interior by peering over the low sections of its parapet wall. The hump of land northeast of the pig farm is Comino's highest point, and the garigue habitat here supports a hugely diverse array of plants, including musty scented wild thyme, rotund tree spurges that look like bonsai trees, as well as capers, which sport beautiful white and purple blooms in spring, and St John's wort with its pea-sized yellow flowers. The flora here is all the more impressive when you consider that it has only dry pockets of soil accumulated in the rugged rocky surface in which to grow – given their fragile hold and slow growth, avoid stepping on the plants.

From here, you can continue towards Santa Marija Bay along the cliffs, or head towards it via the road that cuts inland from the pig farm. The road runs through **Wied L-Aħmar**, Comino's most fertile land, fringed by native carobs, olives, almonds and Aleppo pines; in the spring, the uncultivated portions of the valley are covered with a carpet of bright yellow cape sorrel flowers.

Santa Marija Bay

Wied L-Aħmar opens into Santa Marija Bay, where the rough road traverses the bay's small strip of sand. With inviting turquoise water, Santa Marija Bay is an ideal spot for a picnic or a day by the sea. There's some good snorkelling to be had among the rocks towards the outer reaches of the bay. On the other side of the headland that encloses the bay (and not accessible from land) is a popular dive site known as Santa Marija Cave, renowned for its silvery shoals of docile bream; all Gozo-based diving centres (see p.169) organize dives to the site.

Our Lady's Return from Egypt

On the southern flank of Santa Marija Bay is a pink-coloured outpost built by the Knights in 1743 and now housing Comino's police station. Some 50m behind this, a dirt road leads to the diminutive fourteenth-century chapel of Our Lady's Return from Egypt (open for services on Sat

▼ SANTA MARIJA BAY

▲ OUR LADY'S RETURN FROM EGYPT

at 6pm, and Sun at 6.30am). Shaded by cypresses and a palm tree, and with timber doors and windows and three bells dangling inside stone hoops, the simplicity of its design, typical of medieval Malta's vernacular architecture, gives the building a striking, evocative appearance. Continuing along the road beyond the chapel you can turn right at the first crossroads to go to San Niklaw Bay, or press on to the Blue Lagoon.

Hotel

Comino Hotels and Bungalows

San Niklaw Bay ⓣ21/529821, ⓦwww.cominohotels.com. April–Oct only.

The only accommodation on Comino, and perfect if you're looking for isolation. The en-suite rooms are spacious, with a/c, TVs and balconies. Watersports facilities include diving and windsurfing, and there are ten tennis courts and a gym as well as restaurants and bars. The hotel also rents detached bungalows – some of which have four or five beds – in Santa Marija Bay. Doubles €130, breakfast and dinner included.

Essentials

Arrival

International flights arrive at Malta International Airport, around 8km south of Valletta. There's a taxi stand at the arrivals terminal; approximate fares are €14 to Valletta, €19 to Sliema and St Julian's, €23.50 to Buġibba and €30 to Ċirkewwa; you should always negotiate the price in advance. Bus #8 runs from the stop just outside the arrivals terminal to the main bus station in Valletta (daily 5.30am–10pm, every 30min; €0.50). There's also a direct bus to the Gozo ferry at Ċirkewwa (€5) with between 8 and 12 trips daily depending on season; for a schedule call ⓣ22109001 or email ⓔbusservice@gozochannel.com.

Information and websites

Local and overseas offices of the Malta Tourism Authority (ⓦwww.visitmalta.com) supply leaflets on sights and activities, as well as free (but somewhat inadequate) maps and an annual calendar of events; staff can help with basic queries, and all local offices have lists of accommodation options. In some offices (such as at the airport), they can help you book accommodation on the spot.

Tourist offices in Malta

Airport Arrivals hall ⓣ23/696073. Daily 10am–9pm.
Valletta Freedom Square ⓣ21/237747. Mon–Sat 8.30am–6pm, Sun 8.30am–2pm.
Gozo Tiġrija Palazz, on Triq Ir-Repubblika, Rabat ⓣ21/561419. Mon–Sat 9am–5pm, Sun 9am–12.30pm.

Overseas tourist offices

UK Unit C, Park House, 14 Northfields, London SW18 1DD ⓣ020/8877 6990, ⓔoffice.uk@visitmalta.com.
Ireland Plunkett Communications, 4 Morehampton Rd, Dublin 4 ⓣ01/6781460 ⓔinfo@plunkettcommunications.com.
Australia World Aviation Systems, 403 George St, Sydney NSW 2000 ⓣ02/9321 9154, ⓔoffice.au@visitmalta.com.

Websites

ⓦ**www.aboutmalta.com.** Daily news, weather forecasts, special features and directories of Malta-related sites on everything from the economy to the environment; they also have accommodation listings.
ⓦ**www.gozo.com.** Covers Gozo more extensively with information on sights, boat trips and town feasts, a business directory, and listings of self-catering apartments and villas for rent.
ⓦ**www.searchmalta.com.** A search engine with extensive links and features.
ⓦ**www.visitmalta.com.** Malta Tourism Authority's website and the best general online resource, it provides a glossy overview of the islands, and useful practical information on transport and accommodation, as well as a calendar of events.

Transport

Buses

With an extensive and cheap network of buses, it's relatively easy to explore Malta via public transport; services in Gozo are fewer and inadequate (see p.164 for information on Gozo's public transport). Malta's buses are a bewildering mix of vehicles, and some of them are creaky and rattling postwar buses which can be slow and uncomfortable – the good news is that the longest journey is only fifty minutes. Virtually all services originate from and return to the main Valletta bus station (see p.47), and there are two other small bus stations in Sliema (see p.72) and Buġibba (see p.105) that offer direct services to popular places such as the Three Cities, Mdina and Rabat, Marsaxlokk, Ċirkewwa (for the Gozo ferry), and the beaches of Għajn Tuffieħa and Golden Bay. Services from the Valletta bus station start at 5.30am and stop between 9pm and 11pm, depending on the route (services to Paċeville run later; see p.76). Fares for services starting from and returning to Valletta are €0.50, while all direct services from Sliema and Buġibba, as well as night services to Paċeville, cost €1; all fares are paid on board. Bus passes for unlimited travel are sold at the bus stations; they're valid for one, three, five or seven days and cost €3.50, €9.50, €12 and €14 respectively.

Although buses are numbered, destinations along the route are not listed, so finding out if a route goes where you want to can be difficult, and bus stops do not display their location (however drivers are normally happy to tell you where to get off). Bus schedules and maps of bus routes are available from tourist offices and the bus stations, and at Ⓦwww.atp.com.mt (you can download a bus map). For more information contact the Public Transport Association on Ⓣ21/250007, 250008 or 250009.

Car rental

Renting a car is more convenient than relying on buses, but the downside, aside from the expense, is hit-and-miss signage, poor road conditions and chaotic local driving habits. Nonetheless, a car can be cheaper than taking taxis if you plan to go out at night a lot, particularly if you're staying in northwest Malta, which is a fair way from the nightlife at Paċeville or Valletta. To rent a car or a motorbike, you'll need to present a valid driving licence, and must be over 21. You may also need to show your passport, and some firms ask for a cash deposit or credit card imprint. An optional extra €5 to €7 for comprehensive insurance cover is worth considering given Malta's high accident rates; otherwise, damage to the vehicle can incur the insurance excess of €350. Average rates for a four-door car are about €23 per day, and are usually discounted if you rent for longer than five days. Before renting, it's worth checking with your airline to see if they offer discounts on car rental. Reputable companies are listed below; all can arrange for cars to be picked up and left at the airport or other locations, and in all cases you can get a quote, book and pay via their website.

Car rental companies

Budget 50 Msida Seafront, Msida Mexico Buildings, Triq Żimelli, Marsa Ⓣ21/233668, Ⓦwww.budget.com.mt.

Hertz United House, 66 Triq Il-Gżira, Gżira Ⓣ21/314630; airport office Ⓣ21/232811, Ⓦwww.hertz.com.mt.

Ⓦwww.malta-car-hire.com Umbrella company for a number of affiliate companies throughout the islands.

Mayjo Car Rentals Triq Fortunato Mizzi, Rabat, Gozo Ⓣ21/556678, Ⓦwww.mayjo.com.mt.

Rabat Garage 2 Triq Kola Xagħra, Rabat Ⓣ21/453975, Ⓦwww.rabatgarage.com.mt.

Swansea 102 Triq Manoel De Vilhena, Gżira Ⓣ21/313261 or (freephone) Ⓣ80073143.

Motorbike and cycle rental

Motorbike rental appears to be on the way out following a sharp rise in insurance premiums that have made it uncompetitive. An 80cc moped in high season now costs as much as an economy car, although prices in low season can drop to about €16. At the time of writing only On Two Wheels in Gozo (36 Rabat Road, Marsalforn; ⓣ21/561503 or ⓣ99421621) had plans to continue renting motorbikes and mountain bikes. If you rent a motorbike on Gozo, bear in mind that bends can be slippery (because of gravel or wet conditions) and watch out for potholes.

On Two Wheels is also the only place to rent **mountain bikes** on the islands (€7.50 for a single day; €5 for multi-day rent). Although rural areas of Gozo can be pleasant to explore by bike, and distances are short, the topography is hilly and the summer heat can be exhausting.

Taxis

Official taxis are white and have their registration number painted on the side of the car. There are plenty of strategically located taxi stands in the central areas, airports and ports, and in Paċeville and some of the tourist circuits. Though taxis have meters, they're rarely used, and fares are fairly arbitrary – in most cases, drivers will try to squeeze as much money out of you as possible, and it's acceptable to haggle forcefully. Fares are expensive: expect to pay at least €12 from Valletta to Sliema, or from the Gozo ferry at Mġarr Harbour to Rabat, Gozo. After the buses have stopped running at about 11pm, prices generally go up by about a third. Several companies offer a 24-hour service – good options include Wembley's in St Julian's (ⓣ21/374141 or 374242); Swansea in Sliema (ⓣ21/313261 or ⓣ99475090); Zephyr Garage in Mosta (ⓣ21/434031 or ⓣ99487192); Rabat Garage in Malta's Rabat (ⓣ21/453975 or ⓣ99471921). Haggling won't work with these operators; you'll be quoted a fixed fare when you call. There are two taxi stands in Gozo: at Mġarr Harbour and near the bus station in Rabat, but at night you won't find taxis anywhere and you would have to pre-arrange with a chauffeur-driven car – try Mayjo in Rabat, Gozo (ⓣ21/556678 or ⓣ99423065).

Festivals and events

The highlights of the Maltese festival calendar are the effervescent summer *festas* that commemorate each town's patron saint. You can find info on all festivals and events in the yearly calendar of events available from the tourist offices, or online at ⓦwww.visitmalta.com.

Catholic town feasts

The 82 Catholic feasts organized annually by each town to commemorate its parish saint are unmissable if you're in Malta between June and September. For most Maltese, their town's *festa* is the cultural event of the year, a three-day affair of brass band concerts, fireworks and general merriment alongside adulation of the local patron saint. Everyone dresses in their finest clothes, streets are decorated with colourful lights, statues and tapestries, and church interiors are decked out with damask, silverware and crystal chandeliers.

Probably copied from Sicilian traditions, the feasts originated in the late seventeenth century as modest

The best feasts

For fireworks

The two-hour show in Lija (see p.101), on the eve of the feast every August 5, is an artistic and logistical feat. Mqabba also mounts an exceptional show on August 14.

For church interiors

Head for St Lawrence in Vittoriosa (see p.67) on August 8, or St Mary's in Xagħra (see p.142) on September 8.

For tradition

On June 28 between sunset and sunrise, thousands enjoy a traditional rabbit meal and take in live folk music at Il-Buskett in Rabat (see p.94).

For rivalry

Hamrun, which celebrates its feast on the first weekend after August 7, sees two rival brass band clubs march through the streets, dressed in blue and red respectively, hollering slogans at each other and hurling paint at the facades of the rival club. Two feasts in Gozo's Rabat (San Ġorġ in mid-July and Santa Marija on August 15; see p.135) feature similar scenes, when activists beat and burn effigies of the rival band club.

For Catholic adulation

On August 15, at Gozo's Citadel (see p.136), thousands of devotees hail the Madonna with feverishly rapt singing as the statue reaches the church at around 10pm.

celebrations involving bonfires, firecrackers, music, Catholic ritual and Mass. They evolved into their present form during the nineteenth century, when parishioners invested more money and energy and developed their pyrotechnic displays into a professional industry, and continue to increase in popularity – donations for the feasts swell year after year. Each parish mobilizes a huge effort to organize its annual feast. Funds come from door-to-door donations or fund-raising events (the average household donates at least €20 annually), and all the preparation is carried out by volunteers. This makes the feasts a collective endeavour of each town, a yearly ritual that serves as a reaffirmation of the centrality of the Catholic Church in community affairs.

Evoking passion, pomp, pride, romance and a sense of sharing common values, the pathos of the feasts generates community spirit, but also brings out the rivalry inherent in Maltese society – each town competes to create the most spectacular event, while there's also intense rivalry between different band clubs within the same town. The most visible aspect of the feasts is the fabulous firework displays that round off each town's event. Some 800 volunteer pyrotechnists dedicate their spare time all year round to make the fireworks (the combined value of the fireworks that they produce is €12 million, almost equal to the revenue generated by the agricultural industry), and some of the displays put on here are among the best in the world (top pyrotechnic outfits in Malta regularly win international firework competitions).

Although feast-related activities (community games, barbecues and so on) begin about two weeks before the actual date of the feast, the full-scale celebrations only take place in the last three days, generally Fri to Sun, when the town square fills up with people, stalls sell refreshments and the bars stock up. On the Fri and Sat evenings, a brass band plays in the town square, while a second band leads a procession headed by the statue of the patron saint, and fireworks explode through the skies. On the main day of the feast, celebrations start with a morning High Mass, followed at noon by a brass-band march when inebriated young people dance wildly and sing the thematic slogans of their parish. Some towns also organize horse races in the afternoon (normally 2–5pm). By 7pm, the brass band heralds the final round of celebrations in the town square by playing more adulatory tunes as another statue of the parish saint comes out of the church. More fireworks are then followed by a final procession with the statue. Throughout, the skies are ablaze with fireworks, which reach a colourful finale as the statue reaches the church. A final brass band march marks the close of the feast.

Carnival

Staged in Valletta and Floriana during the week preceding Lent, the carnival parades organized by the Department of Culture in Valletta and Rabat (Gozo) feature large colourful floats and professional dance troupes that compete for awards. Nadur in Gozo sees more interesting pre-Lenten celebrations which are closer to the mock-revolutionary origins of carnival, in which the underclasses romped through the streets in an unruly event. Although modern influences are evident (you'll see lots of latex Halloween-style masks), the unorganized street theatre and performances are still driven by the original spirit, and many of the costumes are highly creative, deliberately farcical parodies of the powers-that-be. In the bars, traditional bands – playing tambourines, the accordion and obscure instruments, including the *żavżava* (a rustic instrument that produces a *hoomph-hoomph* by amplifying the vibrations of a cat's skin stretched over a drum-like contraption) – work up the wildly inebriated and dancing crowds.

Holy Week

Each Good Friday, many Maltese towns stage sober biblical re-enactments. Starting at dusk, these impressive parades feature Biblical characters and statues representing the Stations of the Cross. The highlight of the parades is the participants dressed in white robes and hoods, and dragging bundles of metal chains or wooden crosses, in penitence and holy self-mortification. The best re-enactments are held in Xagħra (see p.142), Żejtun (see p.123) and Valletta (see p.47). On Easter Sunday towns all over Malta erupt in celebration, and events include sprinting with the statue of the Risen Christ to symbolize Christ's Resurrection – the most raucous events are held in Vittoriosa (see p.64) and Xagħra after morning Mass at around 10am.

Notte Bianca – Lejl Imdawwal

Normally held on the first Saturday of October, this event is modelled on similar events called White Nights in Europe. The idea, in Malta, is to have one night of cultural and entertainment activities in Valletta. The events, which start at around 8pm and wind down by 4am, are numerous and varied. There are several concerts, one held at a main stage in Freedom Square (normally featuring mid-range European bands), and others, including Maltese traditional singing and jazz, held in select bars or smaller squares. Other happenings include art installations and exhibitions, as well as a range of other events based on traditional festivals, including a re-enactment of a medieval market. Equally importantly, many historic buildings not normally open to the public (including Auberge de Castille, where the prime minister's office is situated) are open for the night, and there are also free thematic tours of Valletta (such as "Sex and the City" – a tour of the former red light district). Bars and restaurants join the fray by offering special deals for the night; most of them set tables on the streets. It all makes for a great night out, and despite the tens of thousands that descend on Valletta for the event, transport arrangements are efficient – buses shuttle between Valletta and various central towns, and parking isn't that hard to find either. You can get more information at Ⓦ www.nottebiancamalta.com.

Christmas

In such an intensely Catholic country, Christmas sees many parishes, as well as individuals, put up impressive mechanized cribs, or more artistic variations of cribs. Venues come and go; watch out for signs advertising cribs (called *presepju* in Maltese). The displays are more ubiquitous in Gozo, where many residents put up window-displays in their homes – ranging from simple affairs of baby Jesus in a crib and lit by twinkling lights, to more sumptuous and elaborate arrangements. There are also more cribs on show in Gozo, and the best ones are the two in Xagħra – a mechanized crib in the church parochial centre, and a more artistic version, using life-size figures dressed in period garb, in the unused wartime shelter underneath the town square. The religious build-up climaxes on Christmas Eve when most Maltese attend a ritualized version of High Mass at midnight.

Sports and outdoor activities

Scuba diving and watersports

Watersports outfits operate on many of the islands' main beaches between May and Oct, and offer anything from parasailing, waterskiing, wake-boarding or jet-skiing to canoes and kayaks for rent; many also have speedboats for rent.

Malta's waters offer some of the best scuba diving in the Mediterranean, and attract some 50,000 enthusiasts annually. Aside from stunning seascapes (from boulder meadows, gulleys, chimneys and ledges to sheer cliff-drops), underwater visibility is excellent here – 20m in spring and autumn during plankton build-up, and up to 45m between Nov and March – while the mild weather allows year-round diving (water temperatures rise to a peak average of 27°C in summer, and go down to an average of 15°C in winter). Of the three islands, Gozo offers the most spectacular dive sites, especially off Dwejra at the western tip – but the basic rule of thumb is that the further north you go, the better the diving. Lawson and Leslie Wood's *Dive Sites of Malta, Comino and Gozo* contains detailed information (available online and at Sapienza's Bookshop in Valletta; see p.60).

The diving centres scattered throughout the islands are professional outfits affiliated with the major international schools (PADI, CMAS and BSAC etc), and offer all the standard courses plus specialized programmes such as night- or cave-diving, as well as renting out equipment. Five-day open water courses start from around €330, and three-day advanced open water courses start from €220. Most schools also offer taster dives for the uninitiated – instructors take you down to a depth of up to 10m without the need of prior instruction (around €40). You can join the diving centres in escorted or group dives (around €20 per dive, including equipment), or, if you're a qualified diver, you can rent equipment and dive independently – if you're planning independent diving, bear in mind that some dives can be tricky for those not used to local conditions; fatal incidents are reported yearly in caves off Dwejra in Gozo, when silt stirs up and obscures the caves' mouths.

Diving centres

Malta

Dive Systems Tower Point, Tower Rd, Sliema ⓣ21/319123, ⓦwww.divesystemsmalta.com.
Maltaqua Mosta Rd, St Paul's Bay ⓣ21/571873, ⓦwww.maltaqua.com.
Sub-Way Vista Complex, Triq Il-Korp Tal-Pijunieri, Buġibba ⓣ21/572997, ⓦwww.subwayscuba.com.

Gozo

Calypso Diving Centre Triq Marina, Marsalforn ⓣ21/561757, ⓦwww.calypsodivers.com.
Gozo Aqua Sports Rabat Rd, Marsalforn ⓣ21/563037, ⓦwww.gozoaquasports.com.
Moby Dives Triq Il-Gostra, Xlendi ⓣ21/551616, ⓦwww.mobydivesgozo.com.

Snorkelling

The best underwater scenery and the largest concentration of marine life are found in the nooks and crannies along the islands' rocky shores. As well as colourful growths, underwater rocks harbour clusters of spiny sea urchins, inquisitive common octopus and beautiful red starfish. Finger-sized fishes such as blennies, grey triggerfish and connemara suckerfish float in shallow waters, darting away as you get close to explore their variegated colours. Large, silvery shoals of fish are also commonly seen close to the shoreline – these include bream, mullet, silverfish, sand smelt, chromis and wrasse.

Yacht charters

The Maltese islands' coastline – especially the sheer cliffs of southwest Gozo – is far more beautiful from the sea than from any terrestrial perspective, and chartering a yacht allows some fabulous views as well as access to many coves and creeks that are only reachable from the sea. You can also go further afield; some yachts are equipped with plush bedrooms, and can take you anywhere in the Med – popular routes go to Sicily or Greece and back. Prices vary depending on level of service and type of boat – generally speaking, you're unlikely to find anything for less than €250 daily from reputable companies such as S & D Yachts Ltd, Sea Breeze, Triq Giuseppe Cali, Ta Xbiex (ⓣ21/339908, ⓦwww.sdyachts.com), and Sail Away Charters (ⓣ99405610, ⓔmallia1890@yahoo.com). However, best deals are often had from freelance operators – just visit the yacht marina in Msida creek (at the inner mouth of Marsamxett Harbour) or Mġarr Harbour in Gozo (in Gozo, all yacht charters are run by freelance operators).

Hiking

The network of paths that crisscross the Maltese countryside offer ample opportunity for hiking. The best time is winter (Oct–May), when the weather is mild and the landscape green – in summer, you'll find that only early morning or evening walking is comfortable and the parched countryside isn't that appealing. Bear in mind, also, that during autumn and spring (and particularly in April and May), bird-hunters can be a nuisance; besides shattering the peace with shotgun blasts, hunters can get tetchy with strollers, largely because they are aware that non-hunters may disapprove. Although incidents are rare, if you encounter a hunter the most prudent thing to do is to greet him affably and keep going.

We've detailed some short, scenic walks in the guide, but for longer hikes, head to Malta's south coast between Dingli Cliffs and Ras Il-Qammiegħ, or to Gozo's coastal cliffs between Mġarr Ix-Xini and Xlendi, Xlendi and Ras Il-Wardija, and San Blas Bay and Marsalforn. You can also join for free the Ramblers Association (ⓣ99497080, ⓦ www.ramblersmalta.jointcomms.com) on one of the walks – about four monthly – they do between October and May (detailed programmes of walks are on the website). Another possibility is to walk with Malta Outdoors (ⓣ99925439, ⓦ www.maltaoutdoors.com), who organize tailor-made walks, including a four-day trek around Gozo's coast.

Birdwatching

Though Maltese birdlife is constantly threatened by hunters, the islands nonetheless offer fairly good birdwatching during the spring and autumn migrations when Eurasian migratory birds crossing the Mediterranean stop off here. Around 320 species have been recorded in Malta. Most spectacular are the raptor migrations, and you can join seasoned birdwatchers in the annual Raptor Camp – held for three weeks each in Sept and April – whose aim, aside from birdwatching, is to discourage illegal hunting by the presence of birdwatchers in strategic locations. These camps are organized by Birdlife Malta (57/28 Marina Court, Abate Rigard St, Ta' Xbiex; ⓣ 21/347646, ⓦ www.birdlifemalta.org), and participation is free. The Sept season is the most rewarding: hundreds of birds of prey descend on Il-Buskett (see p.94) to roost on brisk migrations days.

For waterbirds, visit Is-Simar Wetland Reserve, a managed habitat of lush reed-fringed waterways that, aside from attracting migrating waterbirds, is also home to nesting reed warblers. Is-Simar, at St Paul's Bay, is open to the public between Nov and May on Sun (10am–4pm; free), and you can also arrange to visit at other times by contacting the warden Charles Coleiro on ⓔ ccol@onvol.net or ⓔ carmel.a.coleiro@gov.mt). Further north, Għadira Wetland Reserve (see p.113) is a more open, brackish wetland.

Rock climbing

The Maltese islands offer exciting climbing at all levels, with cliffs girdling virtually the entire northwest and southwest coasts and numerous stretches of inland cliffs. Many hundreds of climbs have been charted – 1200 routes are detailed in the guidebook *Malta Rock Climbing*, available from Sapienza's in Valletta (see p.60) – and the past few years has seen the bolting of dozens of sports-climbing routes. Malta Outdoors (see above) offers guided climbs or equipment rental. In Gozo and Comino – which offer the best overall climbs, partly because the countryside is less developed – have their own dedicated guidebook published by the specialist company Gozo Adventures (ⓣ 21/564592 or ⓣ 99241171; ⓦ www.gozoadventures.com), an operator that offers all types of guided climbs (or rental of equipment), as well as bouldering, deep-water soloing, and coasteering.

Horse riding

Malta's dramatic northwest coastline around Għajn Tuffieħa is lovely to explore on horseback; head for Golden Bay Horse Riding (ⓣ 21/573360; daily 8am–6pm; €18 per hour) situated in the immediate hinterland of Golden Bay. In Gozo the rural roads and valleys make horse riding even more rewarding; Victor's Horse and Carriage (15 Triq Shase, Xagħra, Gozo; ⓣ 21/559229 or ⓣ 99858194, ⓦ www.vmcarriages.com; variable hours, call in advance) does guided horse riding for €20 per hour, or family tours in a horse-driven vintage-style carriage.

Hands-on farming

Ager Foundation, a non-profit rural development organization, does guided one-day hands-on farming or fishing trips in Gozo. The concept pivots on participation – visitors take part in daily chores at a sheep farm or a crop farm, and learn more about farming in the process. Likewise, guests can join a fisherman fishing near shore with traditional nets and traps, and then afterwards take the catch to a beach in Comino for a barbecue. Another activity is a day-long cookery course in which you learn to prepare various traditional Gozitan dishes. Most activities cost €19 for adults and €10 for children – the exception is fishing, for which prices are €23 and €14 respectively. The price includes pick-up and drop-off at Mġarr Harbour, transport and lunch. For more information visit ⓦ www.agerfoundation.com or call ⓣ 79017017.

Other sports

Marsa Sports Club (MSC) in Marsa (daily 8.30am–11pm; ⓣ 21/233851, ⓦ www.marsasportsclub.com) has seventeen all-weather tennis courts, as well as squash courts, that you can rent for €16 for ninety minutes (€23 after 7pm) – payment also gets you free use of other facilities, including swimming pool and children's playground. The MSC is also home to Malta's only golf course (ⓣ 21/227019, ⓦ www.royalmaltagolfclub.com), an 18-hole par-68 course; clubs can be rented for €18–25 each daily, electric buggy for €38, and a round costs €60 in the summer high season. Fringe spectator sports are also sometimes held in the complex, such as rugby, polo, cricket and archery – call in advance to see what's on.

Cinemas, theatres and casinos

Cinemas

All mainstream cinemas have modern theatres and generally feature Hollywood releases. Tickets cost between €3.50 and €6.50, and most offer discounts before 5pm. Art-house films are aired nightly at St James Cavalier (see p.51).

Citadel Theatre Pjazza Indipendenza, Rabat, Gozo ⓣ 21/559955, ⓦ www.citadelcinema.com. Two screens.

Eden Century Cinemas Triq Santu Wistin, St George's Bay, St Julian's ⓣ 23710400, ⓦ www.edencinemas.com.mt. Seventeen screens.

Embassy Triq Santa Lucia, Valletta ⓣ 21/222225, ⓦ www.embassycomplex.com.mt. Six screens.

Empire Cinema Complex Triq Il-Korp Tal-Pijunieri, Buġibba ⓣ 21/581787, ⓦ www.empirecinema.com.mt. Seven screens.

Theatre

There are four theatres in the Maltese islands: two in Valletta, and two in Rabat, Gozo; the theatre season runs between Oct and May. Check at tourist offices for details of upcoming events, or keep an eye out for posters, as well as listings in local newspapers. Offerings are fairly varied, from mainstream touring productions to plays by Maltese companies, whilst theatres are also used to stage classical music concerts, opera and ballet.

Astra Theatre 9 Triq Ir-Repubblika, Rabat, Gozo ⓣ 21/556256 or 550985, ⓦ www.lastella.com.mt. The largest Baroque theatre in Malta features anything from operas to drama and ballet.

Aurora Opera Theatre Triq Ir-Repubblika, Rabat, Gozo ⓣ 21/559452 or ⓣ 21/562974, ⓦ www.leone.org.mt. A large theatre renowned for excellent operas; it also stages drama and other events such as ballet.

Manoel Theatre Triq It-Teatru L-Antik, Valletta ⓣ 21/246389, ⓦ www.teatrumanoel.com.mt. Built by the Knights in the eighteenth century, Malta's 600-seater National Theatre features drama and concerts.

Theatre in the Round St James Cavalier, Triq Papa Piju V, Valletta ⓣ 21/223200, ⓦ www.sjcav.org. A small theatre with sixty seats arranged around the central stage. Productions range from classical concerts to experimental plays.

Casinos

You'll have to show some sort of identification to prove you're over 18 to visit any of Malta's four casinos listed below; dress code is smart-casual. All casinos offer rows of slot machines, as well as table games such as blackjack, poker, punto banco, roulette and chemin de fer.

Casino di Venezia Ix-Xatt Tal-Birgu, Vittoriosa ⓣ21/805580 ⓦwww.casinodivenezia.com.mt. Mon–Thurs 2pm–2am, Fri & Sun 2pm–4am; some gaming tables start at 6pm on weekends and 8pm on weekdays. Malta's most sumptuous casino is housed in a beautiful building that was originally built as the headquarters of the Knights' naval fleet.

Dragonara *Westin Dragonara Hotel*, St Julian's ⓣ21/382362, ⓦwww.dragonara.com. Mon–Thurs 10am–6am, Fri–Sun 24hr. A lovely setting in a nineteenth-century Neoclassical building.

Oracle Casino *Dolmen Hotel*, Dolmen St, Buġibba ⓣ21/570057, ⓦwww.oraclecasino.com. Mon–Thurs & Sun 10am–4am, Fri & Sat 10am–6am. A large, modern in-hotel casino.

Portomaso Casino *Portomaso Complex*, St Julian's ⓣ21/383777, ⓦwww.portomasocasino.com. Mon–Thurs & Sun 10am–5am, Fri & Sat 10am–6am; gaming tables start at 1pm. Malta's newest, largest and plushest casino.

Directory

Banks and exchange Malta's currency is the euro (see box on p.6 for information on its adoption in 2008). Most banks open Mon to Sat in the morning, and afternoons one or two days a week; in towns, you'll never be more than a ten-minutes' walk from one, and all branches have ATMs (in Gozo, however, there are only ATMs in Rabat, Marsalforn, and Xlendi). Banks offer the best rates for cash or travellers' cheques; exchange bureaux normally charge a higher commission of about three percent, though their opening hours tend to be more convenient, while hotels charge a similar commission and round off the exchange rate to their advantage. All major credit cards – Visa, Mastercard, American Express, Diners, as well as others – are widely accepted by shops, restaurants, hotels and guesthouses and car rental companies.

Costs Malta isn't cheap, and the cost of living is rising. Supermarket prices reach EU averages, and a two-course meal excluding drinks in a restaurant will cost around €21; alcoholic drinks, however, are cheaper than in most European countries. Public transport and entry fees for sights and museums are relatively inexpensive. Accommodation will be your biggest expense: a hostel bunk costs about €7 per night, guesthouses start from €25 for a double room, and €60 will get you an en-suite double room with a/c, phone and TV. The accommodation prices quoted in this guide are the starting rates during peak summer months; these fall substantially in the low season.

Travellers with Disabilities Planning rules have only had to make provision for people with disabilities in the last decade, and facilities generally remain rather poor, though many upmarket hotels have specially equipped rooms. The National Commission for Persons with Disabilities, Ċentru Hidma Soċjali, Triq Braille, Santa Venera (mid-June to Sept 8.30am–1pm; Oct to mid-June Mon–Fri 8.30am–noon & 2–4.30pm ⓣ21/487789 or ⓦwww.knpd.org) is focused on fostering a national framework for people with disabilities, not providing general information, though you can contact them if you're stuck, or need any information and assistance.

Electricity The supply is 240V; plugs are three-pin.

Embassies and consulates UK High Commission, Whitehall Mansions, Ta Xbiex Seafront, Ta Xbiex ⓣ23230000; US Embassy, 3rd Floor, Development House, Triq Sant' Anna, Floriana ⓣ25614000 or ⓣ25614147; Canada Consulate, Damajo House, 103 Triq L-Arċisqof, Valletta ⓣ25523233; Australia High Commission, Villa Fiorentina, Ta' Xbiex Terrace, Ta' Xbiex ⓣ21/338201.

Emergencies and useful numbers For police, ambulance and fire service, call ☎112; for air or sea rescue call ☎21/809279 (☎21/824220 outside office hours, including weekends); for government information service call ☎153 (Mon–Fri 9am–5pm); for flight enquiries call ☎50043333; if you're involved in a traffic accident call ☎21/320202.
Hospitals Mater Dei, University Heights, Msida ☎25454182; Gozo General Hospital, Rabat, Gozo ☎21/561600.
Internet Internet cafés are plentiful in towns and tourist areas; you'll pay around €2.50 an hour.
Laundry There are a handful of strategically located laundries, some with coin-operated machines. Malta's largest company, Portughes, has 21 outlets, including one in Rabat, Gozo; they do pick-ups and deliveries from any address (☎21/444444, ⓦwww.portughes.com).
Pharmacies The islands' many pharmacies open Mon–Sat 9am–7pm; daily newspapers list those that open, on a roster basis, in evenings, Sun and public holidays until 10pm.
Post offices Located in virtually every town in the islands, most open Monday to Saturday from 8am to noon, but the two main offices – in Valletta and Rabat, Gozo – stay open until 4pm. Mail to the UK takes three days to a week, ten days to two weeks to North America, and up to three weeks for Australia and New Zealand.
Public holidays Malta has fourteen public holidays: Jan 1, Feb 10, March 19, Good Friday, March 31, May 1, June 7, June 29, Aug 15, Sept 8, Sept 21, Dec 8, Decr 13 and Dec 25.
Telephones The international dialling code for Malta is +356. There are plenty of telephone booths scattered throughout Malta, but most take phonecards that you buy from stationers and souvenir shops. For international calls, you can save a lot of money by using prepaid calling cards; there are several brands, all offering similar pricing structures, but read the small print as some of them have expiry dates from first use.
Time Malta is one hour ahead of GMT.

Chronology

Chronology

c. 5000 BC ▸ Neolithic people arrive in Malta from Sicily.

3600 BC ▸ The first of the Neolithic temples – now the oldest extant buildings in the world – is constructed.

2500 BC ▸ The Neolithic period comes to an inexplicable and abrupt end.

2000 BC ▸ Bronze-Age settlers inhabit Malta, erecting fortified castles and granaries on ridges and hills.

800–480 BC ▸ The Phoenicians turn the island into a centre for sea trade. Mdina is established as Malta's first town.

480–218 BC ▸ Malta falls under the control of Carthage.

218 BC ▸ After several wars between Carthage and Rome, the latter finally consolidates its rule in Malta.

60 AD ▸ St Paul is shipwrecked in Malta on the way to his trial in Rome, and the first seeds of Christianity on the island are sown.

395–870 AD ▸ After the split in the Roman Empire, Malta falls under Byzantine rule.

870 ▸ Aghlabid Arabs coming from North Africa invade and capture Malta, and Islamic rule begins – a period whose lasting legacy is the development of the Maltese language, and irrigation systems that are still practised today.

1090–1530 ▸ The Normans, after establishing themselves in Sicily, eventually take Malta from the Arabs. In subsequent centuries Malta swings under the influence of various rulers, including the Aragonese, Swabians and Angevins, as well as various regional strongmen and merchants who run the islands as their private fiefdom.

1530 ▸ Charles V of Spain donates Malta to the Knights of St John (now the Knights of Malta) in return for a Maltese falcon every year. The Knights, in retreat after being routed out of Rhodes by the Ottomans, put Malta on the frontline of the Muslim–Christian struggle for supremacy and territory.

1551 ▸ Dragut Rias, an Ottoman general, attacks Malta with his fleet. The Knights repel the attack, and Dragut raids Gozo instead; he breaches the Citadel and 5000 able people – out of a population of 5500 – are kidnapped as slaves.

1565 ▸ Dragut leads a second attack with a massive show of force, but after his death and a war of attrition lasting six months, the Ottoman army is defeated in what's now known as the Great Siege of 1565.

1566 ▸ Work begins on Valletta, Malta's new fortified capital city.

1798 ▸ Aided by treacherous Knights, Napoleon Bonaparte takes Malta in three days of light skirmishes; the Knights are given three days to pack up their personal possessions and leave, and Napoleon loots most of their riches to pay for his wars.

1798 ▸ Three months after the arrival of the French, the Maltese revolt against them. The French retreat to Valletta, and the Maltese insurgents – aided by the British Army – lay siege to Valletta to dislodge the French; it takes two years before the starving French soldiers surrender.

1800 ▸ The British take possession of the islands.

1835 ▸ Britain rules the islands as a colony, and sets up a Maltese Council of Government that advises the British governor.

World War I ▸ Britain turns Malta into a centre for recuperating injured soldiers.

1919 ▸ Protests against the British turn violent, and Britain moves fast to defuse the tension, resulting in a Maltese government with limited autonomy being established in 1921.

World War II ▸ Malta is the headquarters for the British fleet in the Mediterranean, and with Malta-based submarines disrupting the Axis supply routes to Africa, the island is subjected to an intense and prolonged aerial bombardment. By 1942 the Malta is pushed to the brink of starvation and surrender. Finally, in a last-ditch effort, Operation Pedestal brings in supplies that carry Malta through its darkest hour. Malta's contribution to World War II is recognized with the George Cross – the only time the medal has been awarded to a whole nation.

1964 ▸ Malta gains full independence from Britain.

1974 ▸ Malta becomes a Republic.

1979 ▸ The last British and NATO troops are ejected from Malta by Dom Mintoff's fiery socialist government, and Malta formally becomes a Non-Aligned Country.

2004 ▸ Malta joins the European Union as a full member.

2008 ▸ Malta adopts the euro and becomes part of the Schengen visa (open-borders) area within the EU.

Language

Language

Malti ("Maltese" in English) has its roots in the Arabic of western North Africa, but has gathered many words and influences from Italian, English, French, German and Spanish; in fact, it's a mishmash of all these languages. Though a Semitic language, Maltese is written in a Roman script which evolved at the beginning of the twentieth century: Italian was Malta's default language up to 1934, when it was officially replaced by Maltese and English. Virtually everyone speaks good English, and many street signs, shop names, restaurant menus and so on are in English only. Most Maltese speak a hybridized form of Maltese-English in everyday discourse, and a sizeable minority speak English only. Given this situation, the locals don't expect you to attempt to speak Maltese. It's fine to stick to English, and just learn the basics of Maltese pronunciation in order to get to grips with place names.

The Maltese **alphabet** has 29 letters – five vowels (as in English) and 24 consonants (some of which will be new): a, b, ċ, d, e, f, g, ġ, h, ħ, i, j, k, l, m, n, għ, o, p, q, r, s, t, u, v, w, x, ż, z. Pronunciation of most of the letters differs from English, in that emphasis is placed on a drawn-out twang. Instances of markedly unusual pronunciation are listed below.

Maltese pronunciation

ċ as ch in church
e as in bet
g is hard, as in goat
ġ is soft, as in joke
h is silent (except at the end of a word, when it's pronounced like ħ)
ħ is strong and definite, as in hail
i as the English e in bee
j as in yes
għ is silent in most instances
q is a glottal stop – the sound in the beginning and middle of "uh-oh"
x is an English "sh", as in shear
ż is soft, as in zebra
z as in bats

Glossary

auberge an inn of residence for a group of Knights forming a particular *Langue*
baħar sea
bajja bay
bastion triangular outcrop jutting from a line of fortifications to produce a zigzag outline that provided a wide range of fire coverage, and reinforced structural resistance
bieb generic name for a door or doorway; also the gate to a fortified city
bragioli a traditional baked dish of steak with a mincemeat stuffing
cavalier tower within fortifications that acts a raised gun platform and rearguard position
corsair sea-based pirate licensed by the state to carry out piracy against a defined enemy
curtain the main trace of fortifications linking two bastions
dagħjsa boat
demi-bastion a small bastion with one flank
fat ladies generic term for well-endowed stone figures and statues from the Neolithic era

festa generally refers to the three-day summer festivals held to commemorate parish saints; also public holidays
fliegu sea channel
forn bakery
fortizza fort
garigue rugged stretches of rocky landscape with pockets of soil that support plant life
għar cave
għassa tal-pulizija police station
għolja hill
globigerina local limestone used in many Maltese buildings
ġnien garden
Grand Master the absolute ruler of the Knights of Malta
gvern government
gzira island
hobża bread roll or loaf of bread
ħut fish
il-belt city, usually applied to Valletta
ispiżerija pharmacy
karrozza car
kastell castle
kenur traditional stone hearth used for cooking
knisja church
kunsill lokali local council
Langue a grouping of the Knights of Malta, defined by the region from which they originated
luzzu colourful vernacular wooden fishing boats
misraħ square or clearing
mużew museum
parroċċa parish
passiġġatta a walk, particularly an evening stroll by the sea
pastizzi (singular **pastizz**) puff pastry pocket stuffed with mashed peas or ricotta
pjazza town square
posta post office
pulizija police
ravelin triangular defensive outbuilding in front of fortifications
RTO an abbreviation of Reserved To Owner, used by hunters to mark their territory
San or **Sant'** (female **Santa**) saint
sies or **irdum** cliff
sqaq alley
tabib doctor
tal-linja bus
tempju shrine, usually in reference to a Neolithic temple
torri tower
triq street or road
vapur ship
wied valley

small print & Index

A Rough Guide to Rough Guides

In 1981, Mark Ellingham, a recent graduate in English from Bristol University, was travelling in Greece on a tiny budget and couldn't find the right guidebook. With a group of friends he wrote his own guide, combining a contemporary, journalistic style with a practical approach to travellers' needs. That first Rough Guide was a student scheme that became a publishing phenomenon. Today, Rough Guides include recommendations from shoestring to luxury and cover hundreds of destinations around the globe, including almost every country in the Americas and Europe, more than half of Africa and most of Asia and Australasia. Millions of readers relish Rough Guides' wit and inquisitiveness as much as their enthusiastic, critical approach and value-for-money ethos. The guides' ever-growing team of authors and photographers is spread all over the world.

In the early 1990s, Rough Guides branched out of travel, with the publication of Rough Guides to World Music, Classical Music and the Internet. All three have become benchmark titles in their fields, spearheading the publication of a range of more than 350 titles under the Rough Guide name, including phrasebooks, waterproof maps, music guides from Opera to Heavy Metal, reference works as diverse as Conspiracy Theories and Shakespeare, and popular culture books from iPods to Poker. Rough Guides also produce a series of more than 120 World Music CDs in partnership with World Music Network.

Visit www.roughguides.com to see our latest publications.

Rough Guide travel images are available for commercial licensing at www.roughguidespictures.com

Publishing information

This second edition published July 2008 by Rough Guides Ltd, 80 Strand, London WC2R 0RL.
345 Hudson St, 4th Floor, New York, NY 10014, USA.

Distributed by the Penguin Group
Penguin Books Ltd, 80 Strand, London WC2R 0RL
Penguin Group (USA), 375 Hudson Street, NY 10014, USA
14 Local Shopping Centre, Panchsheel Park, New Delhi 110017, India
Penguin Group (Australia), 250 Camberwell Road, Camberwell, Victoria 3124, Australia
Penguin Group (Canada), 10 Alcorn Avenue, Toronto, ON M4V 1E4, Canada
Penguin Group (NZ), 67 Apollo Drive, Mairangi Bay, Auckland 1310, New Zealand
Typeset in Bembo and Helvetica to an original design by Henry Iles.

Cover concept by Peter Dyer.

Printed and bound in China

192pp includes index

A catalogue record for this book is available from the British Library

ISBN 978-1-85828-464-4

1 3 5 7 9 8 6 4 2

Help us update

We've gone to a lot of effort to ensure that the second edition of Malta & Gozo DIRECTIONS is accurate and up-to-date. However, things change – places get "discovered", opening hours are notoriously fickle, restaurants and rooms raise prices or lower standards. If you feel we've got it wrong or left something out, we'd like to know, and if you can remember the address, the price, the phone number, so much the better.

Please send your comments with the subject line "Malta & Gozo DIRECTIONS Update" to Ⓔmail@roughguides.com. We'll credit all contributions and send a copy of the next edition (or any other Rough Guide if you prefer) for the very best emails.

Have your questions answered and tell others about your trip at Ⓦcommunity.roughguides.com

Rough Guide credits

Text editor: Alice Park
Layout: Sachin Tanwar
Photography: Eddie Gerald and Victor Borg
Cartography: Karobi Gogoi
Picture editor: Mark Thomas
Proofreader: Samantha Cook
Production: Rebecca Short
Cover design: Chloë Roberts

The author

Born and bred in Malta, Victor Paul Borg has researched Malta's travel industry better than anyone else. Although he continues to write regularly about Malta for various publications, he also now covers large swathes of the world, Asia particularly, writing long investigative travel features for some of the world's top travel magazines. More of his writing – as well as a blog about his travels and a forum airing intelligent debates about travel – can be found at www.peppermountains.com.

Acknowledgements

Thanks to all the readers who wrote in with suggestions. Apologies for any omissions or misspellings: Tom Butt, Howard Barlow, Sandra Cornbleet, Elisabeth Flaherty, Larry at Morro Bay

Photo credits

All images © Rough Guides except the following:

Front cover: Eye detail of a Luzzu in Marsaxlokk © Alamy
Back cover: The Azure Window, Gozo © Mark Thomas/Axiom
p.11 Grand Masters Palace © Victor Paul Borg
p.11 Hypogeum © Alamy
p.16 Feast fireworks © Victor Paul Borg
p.16 Festival band © Victor Paul Borg
p.17 Christmas © Victor Paul Borg
p.17 Good Friday © Victor Paul Borg
p.20 Grand Masters Palace © Victor Paul Borg
p.20 National Museum © Victor Paul Borg
p.21 Maritime Museum © Victor Paul Borg
p.27 Inquisitor's Palace © Victor Paul Borg
p.29 War Museum © Victor Paul Borg
p.31 The Decapitation of St. John the Baptist, 1608 (oil on canvas) by Caravaggio, Michelangelo Merisi da (15711610) © Co-Cathedral of St. John, Valletta, Malta/ The Bridgeman Art Library
p.31 St Paul's Catacombs © Victor Paul Borg
p.51 National Museum © Victor Paul Borg
p.52 National Museum of Archeology © Victor Paul Borg
p.73 Sliema © Nicholas Pitt/Alamy
p.122 Neolithic Bowl, Hypogeum © Paul Victor Borg

Index

Maps are marked in colour

INDEX